MW00634207

THE
REAL LIVES
OF
TRANSGENDER
AND
NONBINARY
HUMANS

A PUBLISH YOUR PURPOSE ANTHOLOGY

THE REAL LIVES OF TRANSGENDER AND NONBINARY HUMANS

As told to Brandi Lai

Copyright (C) 2021 Publish Your Purpose. All rights reserved.

No part of this publication shall be reproduced, transmitted, or sold in whole or in part in any form without prior written consent of the author, except as provided by the United States of America copyright law. Any unauthorized usage of the text without express written permission of the publisher is a violation of the author's copyright and is illegal and punishable by law. All trademarks and registered trademarks appearing in this guide are the property of their respective owners.

For permission requests, write to the publisher, addressed "Attention: Permissions Coordinator," at the address below.

 **Publish**
Your Purpose

Publish Your Purpose
141 Weston Street, #155
Hartford, CT, 06141

The opinions expressed by the Author are not necessarily those held by Publish Your Purpose.

Ordering Information: Quantity sales and special discounts are available on quantity purchases by corporations, associations, and others. For details, contact the publisher at hello@publishyourpurpose.com.

Edited by: Hunter Liguore, Gail Marlene Schwartz, and Caroline Davis
Cover design by Cornelia Murariu
Typeset by Cornelia Murariu

Printed in the United States of America.

ISBN: 978-1-951591-82-3 (hardcover)
ISBN: 978-1-951591-78-6 (paperback)
ISBN: 978-1-951591-79-3 (ebook)

Library of Congress Control Number: 2021939013
First edition, June 2021

The information contained within this book is strictly for informational purposes. The material may include information, products, or services by third parties. As such, the Author and Publisher do not assume responsibility or liability for any third-party material or opinions. The publisher is not responsible for websites (or their content) that are not owned by the publisher. Readers are advised to do their own due diligence when it comes to making decisions.

Publish Your Purpose is a hybrid publisher of non-fiction books. Our mission is to elevate the voices often excluded from traditional publishing. We intentionally seek out authors and storytellers with diverse backgrounds, life experiences, and unique perspectives to publish books that will make an impact in the world. Do you have a book idea you would like us to consider publishing? Please visit PublishYourPurpose.com for more information.

DEDICATION

This anthology is dedicated
to every brave individual who
has encountered discrimination
and hate in their lifetime.

CONTENTS

ACKNOWLEDGMENTS

Thank you to all of our contributors on this project:

NiK Kacy
Denise Bowker
Tony Ferraiolo
Samantha Lux
Gavriel Legynd
Kai Berzinskas
Braxton T. Fleming
Ashley T. Brundage
Rhodes Perry
Brooke Cooper
Rex E. Wilde
Brandi Lai

Foreword

by Jenn T. Grace

Before publishing books, I was a consultant for lesbian, gay, bisexual, transgender, queer, plus (LGBTQ+) spaces. When I first started in 2006, things were different than they are now. At the time, the word 'gay' was, for the most part, a universal umbrella that many of us within the community were lumped under, regardless of whether or not that was how we identified.

I spent a decade educating the financial service and insurance industries on best practices for working with LGBTQ+ clients and employees. It was during this work, and frankly before, that I could very clearly see inequities when it came to how transgender and nonbinary people were treated.

We often look at allyship as something powerful that straight people can do for the LGBTQ+ community, but what I found to be equally as powerful, was educating folks within the LGBTQ+ space on allyship, in terms of the particular struggles that our trans and nonbinary friends were experiencing. As a self-identified queer woman, I could see that the broader LGBTQ+ movement consistently and overtly left out our transgender family, friends, and colleagues.

It wasn't until years later that the term 'nonbinary' became slightly more commonplace within our lexicon, affording visibility to a wide group of humans who were previously lumped into other letters of the LGBTQ+ alphabet soup.

Back then I made a commitment to be an ally to the trans and nonbinary community. A commitment that I still take seriously. And one I believe every person, LGBTQ+ or straight, should also take seriously. Not only did I want to empower people to be allies, but also to be activists and advocates too.

When I founded Publish Your Purpose in 2015, I made a commitment to serve underrepresented voices. To give those voices power and a stage to share their stories, so they can speak their truth, and impact their communities. And now, as we launch a new subset of what we do, our Publish Your Purpose Anthology series, it couldn't have been more clear that we must kick off this series with *The Real Lives of Transgender and Nonbinary Humans* as our first anthology.

It is my hope, the hope of the contributors of this book, and the hope of the team at Publish Your Purpose, that this book will leave a significant impact on you. The stories shared are meant to empower and uplift the trans and nonbinary community, to show the pathway to hope for those struggling with their identity, and to educate those who may not yet fully understand what these words mean. We welcome you into our hearts, and into our community, to learn and to grow from what you learn.

With Purpose and Impact,

Jenn T Grace

Dear Reader,

The people featured in this book represent a wide spectrum of what it means to be trans and nonbinary. There are people in this book who are parents, each of them with vastly different experiences in their relationships with their families and their children. There are people whose families accept them, who support and help promote the work they are doing, while there are others whose families vehemently reject everything about them. There are people in this book across the spectrum of experiences; some were born in this country, some immigrated to the US. Some have experienced homelessness, racism, and transphobia through so much of their lives. Some are young entrepreneurs, getting their businesses off the ground; some promote the community through local activism; and some just want to make a difference in one person's life, by telling their story in this book.

The thing that binds all of us together is that we all want to share our story in some way. To show more than the stereotypical "trans experience." We are more than just a medical model of how we transition. While that is a part of some of our lives, all our lives extend beyond that. Each of us carry a story inside of us before, through, and beyond transition. Each person represents a broad range of people who have gone through similar yet unique experiences, continuing to grow themselves and the communities they care about.

By telling our stories, we hope to not only foster an understanding of what it means to be trans, but also to provide hope to those who are or were in similar positions to us. To show that, yes, there is "a light at the end of the tunnel." You can make it; you can take an idea that you have and turn it into a business. You can be your authentic self, 100 percent of the time, inspire others around you, and be accepted. You can make it in this world, regardless of who you are.

When you are reading through these stories, consider the lives and lived experiences of the people around you who are trans and nonbinary or who have similar stories. You may know people who are trying to or have already overcome hardships and challenges to be their authentic selves. These experiences are not unique to the trans community. You may find the stories in this book similar to your own or to friends and family. Keep this in mind as you take in each of these stories. These are the real lives and lived experiences of trans and nonbinary people.

These are our stories.

OUR STORIES

NIK KACY

NiK Kacy (they/them) is a gender non-conforming fashion designer and owner of fashion company, NiK Kacy Footwear. They make high quality gender-free shoes that can be worn by anyone. They also founded the first LGBTQ+ fashion week in LA, called Equality Fashion Week. They not only wanted to give back to the LGBTQ+ community by creating visibility and showcasing queer, trans, and BIPOC talent, but they also wanted to develop a platform that provides economic development for the queer community. They hope to grow Equality Fashion Week by taking it on the road to other cities that lack access to queer talent development and fashion.

STRUGGLING IN A NEW HOME

I was born in Hong Kong and lived there for a short period of time in my early childhood. I lived there long enough to form memories of my first family there and to learn Cantonese, my first spoken language. I spent a lot of time with my birth father's side of the family while growing up, but things quickly changed.

My mom first brought me over to the US for a summer when I was about five years old; two years later, my parents ended up getting a divorce. I had only just begun to build a life with the family, friends, and people that I knew; suddenly that was ripped away. After the divorce, my mom and I moved permanently to New York to live with her side of the family. We moved into a triplex with my maternal grandparents and my aunt and uncle. With this distance between us, my birth father dropped out of my life. We would exchange letters every now and then, but he wasn't physically present throughout my growing up years.

Now I was in a foreign country with my mom's family, who were strangers and who didn't speak Cantonese, torn from the only home I had known, and I couldn't even communicate with anyone. I had to learn two new languages when I moved to New York: English, obviously, but also Mandarin, to speak with my mom's side of the family.

At school, I was the Asian kid who didn't speak the language, and I was bullied constantly and cruelly because of it. It was horrible, being made fun of day in and day out, and I wondered why this was happening to me. I was only seven years old at the time, forced to endure the other kids' cruelty. The Asian culture mentality teaches you to be the best at something and be strong, so it was weak to be bullied. I remember being in the bathroom in the middle of this circle of kids who were pushing me and calling me names like "chink" while making fun of my eyes. I couldn't respond because I didn't speak English and I had no idea what to do to defend myself. I just remember feeling like I was at the mercy of everyone there, begging them to stop but having no one there to help me.

My mom wasn't around a lot, and by the time I was seven years old, I was questioning why I was born. *Why did my parents get together, have me, and then leave me? Why was I forced to suffer and go through all of this pain?* I felt unwanted by my family and by the kids around me. I felt alone and isolated. I was forced to try and fend for myself when I was in school.

Finally I realized I had to become a bully in order to survive. It was eat or be eaten, and I was tired of always being a victim, someone to pick on and make fun of. In third grade, about two years after starting grade school in New York, I chopped off my hair and became a total tomboy. I did everything that the boys were doing. I became one of the best baseball players in the yard. Nobody would fuck with me because I was not gonna take it.

It was gradual but, as my English improved, I began to make more and more friends and hung out with the "popular" kids, sitting with the pretty girls at lunch and playing ball with the cool boys during recess. Walking home from school every day with my "pack," nobody bothered me anymore.

One time, during recess in the yard, this kid named Nelson was swinging this wiffle bat and it hit me. I grabbed the bat and started hitting him with it. Granted, it was a lightweight, plastic wiffle bat, so it didn't really hurt him, but we were both called into the principal's office afterwards. I was actually very close to the principal because she always helped me out when I was struggling.

I didn't end up getting in trouble but Nelson did, because he was the one who started it. But I spoke up on his behalf, saying that it was an accident and that we were good. From that point on, we actually ended up becoming friends. That was a pivotal moment, when I acknowledged to myself that I was not born a bully. I thought I had to be a bully in order to survive, but what I learned was that just because you're the victim does not mean you need to become a bully to help yourself.

EARLY IDENTITY: CULTURE, GENDER, AND FAMILY DYNAMICS

When I was around eight or nine years old, I remember I was with my little cousin. My mom and I were giving him a bath and I saw that his body was different than mine. I was surprised and I thought, *Well, why don't I have one of those?* That was one of the first times I realized I was different. When I saw how different our bodies were, I knew that his body was the one I was meant to have. And that made me realize I was different, not just in body and gender but in a way that you can't explain because you've never heard anybody talk about it before. There is no reference for what that difference is, when your insides don't match your outsides, like you're in the wrong body. In addition, he was treated much better than I was, like he was the golden child. I had to do all of the chores. I washed the dishes, served the food, and cleaned the house while he just got to play. In my head, I had thought we were the same. I was a boy just like him, so why was I being treated differently?

My cousin, born male, was going to carry the family name, but I don't know how much of a role culture played in how differently they treated us, on top of the differences between our genders. The irony was that while I hated my life, my little cousin wanted to be just like me. He came to look up to me and wanted to follow me wherever I went and do whatever I did. When I did the dishes, he would come "assist" me, or if I set the table, he would help out. Nobody required him to do any of that, but he chose to do the work. For me, it was never a choice.

Throughout the years, I became resigned to my fate as a girl. When puberty hit and my boobs started showing up, I was mortified. I hated them and, even worse was the fact that I was the most well-endowed in my family. My mom used to joke that she wished she could have them and I would reply, "Please, take them." When I got my first period, I wanted to die. I couldn't understand why my body was cursed to be all the things I dreaded most. As my body developed, so did my resentment towards being treated differently because I'm a girl and there wasn't anything I could do to change that. I had to accept the gender role that was being placed on me, even if I didn't conform to what a girl should wear or do. I remember every time my mom put me in a dress, I would have the worst tantrums. At the time, all I knew was that I hated dresses but I couldn't clearly communicate why. When you look at pictures of me as a child in a dress, there's rarely a smile. Something inside me knew, even as a little child, that it didn't feel right.

I also was struggling with two facets of Asian culture that I experienced in my family. Asian culture emphasizes discipline and also belittling, especially kids, for any imperfections. Growing up, I was constantly being told I was fat and that created much insecurity and self-hatred. I wasn't pretty enough and family members would constantly compare me to my mom. Here she was, this beautiful woman, and there I was, this tomboy who looked like her complete opposite. My grandma would tell me all the time how I looked like, walked like, and acted like my birth father. Even though I barely remembered anything about him, it always felt like an insult: I'm just like my no-good father who didn't treat my mom right.

I could never win in my family's eyes. I couldn't play or exercise a lot because I was forced to study, but I was still always blamed for being fat. And yet, if I didn't finish my plate at the table, I wasn't allowed to leave. I never did enough and I was never good enough.

So I tried to overcompensate. I performed exceedingly well in school. I threw myself into extracurricular activities and tried to have as many friends as possible. I tried to prove to my family and the world that I was good enough, but even after the accolades, achievements, and friends, I still felt empty and unworthy. I didn't feel good enough for my family or those around me. I didn't even feel good enough for myself.

MORE HARDSHIP: A BREAK-IN

My struggles continued in school and at home. To top it off, when I was in sixth grade, my family's home was robbed. It was an average day and someone knocked on the door asking for my uncle, claiming he was delivering a refrigerator. My heart sank the moment that I opened the door because when he looked at me, he seemed surprised to find a kid. He looked to the left and right to see if there was anyone around, and I knew that that was not a normal reaction.

His hand slid into the top of the box and pulled out a machete. He pushed me inside, forced me against the wall, duct taped my mouth, and put the knife against my neck. I still have a scar from that knife wound to this day. Two other guys came in. One put a gun to my head and asked who was upstairs. I remember thinking to myself, *You dumbasses. You duct taped my mouth; how am I supposed to answer?!*

I did try to answer a few times before they finally just pushed me up the stairs. My grandmother was upstairs, yelling through the door, asking me what was happening and if I was okay. We were in a triplex and nobody was home on the first or second floor. When we got toward the final landing, she realized what was happening and I still remember her face of shock and fear. My grandfather was in the back of that apartment, where there were two bedrooms at the end of the hallway—my grandparents and my mom's. He was with my little baby cousin, holding her. The robbers muscled their way in and tied us all up, my grandmother, my grandfather, and me. They pushed us all into my mom's room and turned over the whole house. I could tell that my grandparents were nervous because they were breathing heavily but luckily, I was the only one who got hurt. The men took all of my mom and grandma's jewelry, and once they had turned over the house, they ran away. Looking back, it was fortunate I looked so boyish. I always wonder how things would've been different if I had been dressed femininely. What would have happened to me, and would the robbers have done anything worse?

To this day, we still don't really know who the men were and how they knew that the only people who would be home were a kid and two older people. We questioned my uncle after the incident but he was kind of an asshole and blamed me for opening the door in the first place. Although our questions were never answered, the incident left more than a visible scar on me. I'm now more cautious about my surroundings and I'm very guarded about personal safety and who is around me. From an early age, I learned what it meant to be a crime victim, which shaped my perspective of the world growing up.

I continued to struggle as I made my way through middle and high school. After our home invasion, my grandfather's health took a turn and eventually he passed from complications with his breathing. We moved in with my mom's sister and I was very fortunate that my mom's fiancé (who later became my stepfather and whom I consider my "dad") stepped in and offered to pay for my schooling at a private school. My dad was this Irish-German New Yorker who was from Brooklyn and had a thick New York accent. He met my mom when she was working at my uncle's restaurant in New York City. They dated for a few years and were engaged for a very long time. I spent most of my youth being kind of a brat to him because to me, nobody was good enough for my mom. But he loved my mom a lot and cared for me and my grandma unconditionally. I am very blessed to have had a dad like him.

The home invasion had left me traumatized and the loss of my grandfather made me feel like I needed to work even harder to be a better version of myself. I remember praying in my room at an altar I made for my grandpa the night he passed. I promised him that I was going to do better, that I would study harder and be a good grandkid to my grandma, so he needn't worry. I had carried so much guilt from opening the door for the home invasion, even though it was my grandma who sent me down, and there was no way I could have prevented it. I wanted to be worthy in the eyes of others, while also being in charge of my own life, to not be a victim any longer. However, I continued questioning my identity for years.

After I graduated high school, I went to NYU for exactly one day: orientation. My best friend from elementary school and I both got accepted and we were excited to attend the same university together. However, on that day at orientation, we were told to remember the numbers we were assigned because from that day forward, we were those numbers. I remember feeling tired of being another statistic, another number in a sea of people. I think at that moment I knew that the better option for me in order to build the future I wanted was leaving home and attending a school where the student/teacher ratio was lower, which would be more conducive to my growth. I looked at my friend and she knew.

"You're going to Pepperdine," she said, and I replied, "Yes."

Pepperdine had offered me a full scholarship and financial aid package and was in beautiful Malibu, across the country where I could break away from "traditions" and really find myself. It was not easy to tell my mom that I was moving to California, but deep down my gut told me it was the right choice. I had no family or friends out there, but I think my subconscious craved the freedom to search for who I was meant to be.

Once I got to Pepperdine, it was immediately an incredible experience because for the first time in my life, everyone around me was also having the experience of being new and different. I was around people from all over the world, all on their first day at school. It was completely liberating. I could eat as much or as little as I wanted. I could wear what I wanted. I had complete freedom to do as I pleased. I quickly made friends and became involved with the international students, extracurricular activities, clubs, and a mentoring program for kids from other countries. In my sophomore year, I applied to a Japanese exchange program, since my minor was Japanese and I was VP of the university's Japanese Club.

But even with all of my involvements, I was still struggling with my identity. *Why was I born? Why was I given this life?* Spending time in Japan offered a perfect opportunity to think very differently about these questions.

SOCIETY AND CULTURE
**CONDITIONED ME
INTO THINKING THAT
I HAD TO ACCEPT
MYSELF AND MY BODY
UNCONDITIONALLY,**
EVEN IF IT HURT
MY SOUL.

I was accepted to the program and was assigned to a very progressive host family. My host mom was older than my host dad (which was unusual in that culture), and they liked to dance and do crafts. I couldn't have asked for a more perfect family who matched my demeanor and outlook. They had twin sons who I became very close to, and still to this day I consider them my brothers, my family.

While in Japan, I had the opportunity to build a closeness with the four other American kids participating in the exchange program. We went to school together every day and studied at the Japanese university. We went to bars and traveled together, partied and explored. It was a kind of comfort for me to have that closeness but still maintain some distance. I became very close with one of those classmates, and I was able to share many philosophical conversations with her. During this time of exploration, both culturally in a new land and psychologically in my own mind and heart, I came to realize that living in the body I was in was too hard. I had hidden my sexuality and identity all my life and I hadn't figured out how to process why I felt different. I knew I was blessed: I had a good home, education, loving friends and family. I thought I shouldn't be feeling such pain, but I was, and I ultimately felt I shouldn't have been born. I had con-cluded that, although we don't get to decide to be born into this world, we always have the choice to leave it.

This was a moment where I thought, *Either I'm going to end my life or figure out the reason why I'm still here.* Then there was a shift while I was in Japan, after I tried to harm myself during a drunken night in a hotel. I woke up the next morning, unaware of my attempted suicide. The school admins for the exchange program and my classmates were all concerned, while I had no clue. It was not until I realized my wrists were wrapped and they told me what happened that something inside told me I was still here for a reason, that I needed to keep going as myself and for myself. I needed to truly live as myself and embrace everything that I was, unapologetically. After our school trip was over and I returned to my host family's home, I took some incense and burned it into my hand because I wanted to make sure I had a reminder for myself, every day, that this was my choice and I was going to follow through with that choice. I decided to live authentically as myself, to figure out what that means and to follow wherever my path may take me.

REBIRTH

In high school, I had started to paint. An art teacher, Mr. Hullfish, had let me take home the old white window shades of the school after I asked if I could, since they were throwing them out. I cut them to pieces and he taught me how to stretch them into wood frames to make canvases. He was incredibly patient and kind and I owe a lot of my bravery in starting my artistic endeavors to him, as well as my other art teacher, Sister Donna. Unfortunately, Mr. Hullfish succumbed to pancreatic cancer shortly after my class with him, but he made a permanent impression on me. The main theme in my paintings was rebirth.

When I was in Japan, I practiced calligraphy, and I realized the kanji, or Japanese character, for the word 'birth' ( ) came from the pictograph of a pregnant woman praying. That held such deep meaning for me that I've been attached to the word 'rebirth' ever since. I have a collection of pieces now that are all about rebirth, and I have the word tattooed on my body because that moment was literally my rebirth. The moment I burned incense into my hand was the moment I began birthing myself, the person I want to be and am

The Real Lives of Transgender and Nonbinary Humans

going to become. I didn't know what that person was going to be like, but at least it was on my terms.

In that moment, I recognized that I didn't have much hope that I could leave this world better than I found it. The idea of "hope for the world" is something that's been stuck with me since I was a kid. I watched the movie *Seventh Sign*, set in the apocalypse. The main character is pregnant and it's basically about her hope for her child and for the world. The world would end if she didn't find true hope but because she did, her hope saved her child and the world. When I watched that movie as a child, it left an imprint on me. I also wanted to have enough hope to save the world.

So when it came down to that moment of deciding whether to die or to be reborn as myself, my guiding mission and purpose was to live authentically and to give back to my communities, driven by hope for myself and the world. I want to live authentically, to inspire and to encourage others to do the same. Now this is the path I walk and how I choose to live since my rebirth.

When I got back from Japan, I came out to my friends as a lesbian. I started going out in the gay community, surrounding myself with queers, and immersing myself in lesbian culture. I put myself in quintessential lesbian spots, like Little Frida's Coffee House and The Normandie Room in West Hollywood, which helped me get a foothold in the community. There was even a period of time where I was the door person for one of the most well-attended lesbian nights. I got to meet everyone, since they all had to pass through me to get in.

Thinking back to my coming out experience, I remember fondly how I thought nobody knew, only to realize that everyone suspected. No one was really that surprised when, one fateful night while waiting for a table at some restaurant, a group of my friends and I played Truth or Dare. My roommate asked if I'd ever kissed a girl, and I remember being caught off guard but eventually answered "Yes." Apparently, they all suspected but were waiting for me to come out and tell them. It was great to have their support and know that coming out wasn't something I needed to worry about.

Once I realized my friends weren't going to desert me, I continued to dive into the gay community. About a year later when my mom came to California for my graduation, I came out to her as well. I was so worried what her reaction would be, but she was supportive. However, she did tell me, "I have a secret as well." So we exchanged secrets. At the time, it felt like she stole my thunder. I was so nervous before we talked and then it turned out to be for nothing. I realize in hindsight that her way of responding showed that my coming out wasn't a big deal and that by sharing her secret at the same time, she was letting me know that we are all united in commonality as humans.

NONBINARY

Life went on after graduation. I went to Singapore briefly but ended up moving back to LA because I knew I needed to find myself here. When I came back, I continued to be as active as I could in the community. Being immersed and surrounded by queer people helped me feel I had a home and family and community. I wanted to be involved with every LGBTQ+ community organization and nonprofit in the area...and may have burnt myself out trying to be everywhere at once.

But most importantly, I was on the cusp of a burgeoning nonbinary movement in LA. Because I was surrounded by so many trans and nonbinary folks, I happened to hear many educators speak. I attended a lot of classes and sessions and learned a lot about language, terminology, and how to educate people about trans and nonbinary identities.

As I started to understand and gain language to describe myself, I experienced this internal conflict of having to teach myself how to love myself while feeling like I wasn't whole or comfortable in my body. I'd look in the mirror and feel that I loved myself, that I was a competent human being, but when I'd put on a shirt, I'd feel inadequate. I'd go back and forth constantly, wondering why it was that every time I looked in the mirror and I saw my chest, I always thought, *That's not my body.*

When I'd have sex and the person touched my chest, I would tense up. If I got a compliment on my boobs, I'd cringe. As much as I was an advocate of loving and accepting yourself and not changing to fit an ideal, I also couldn't feel comfortable and love myself with the body I had. I waited to transition because, for so long during this journey of finding myself, I really wanted to be authentic and content with who I was. I thought that included accepting my body as it was.

It took me so long to finally figure out that it was not inauthentic to want to have top surgery or to medically transition. Society and culture conditioned me into thinking that I had to accept myself and my body unconditionally, even if it hurt my soul. But the truth was, no matter how happy or positive my attitude was, I always dreaded my body. I never felt comfortable in clothes and really hated getting my period. I told my mom when I was seven years old, I never wanted to give birth. I knew even at that age that giving birth was not something I felt good or natural about. So in my late 30s, I finally gave myself permission to be truly authentic by augmenting my outside to fit my inside.

Leading up to my surgery, people would constantly ask me, "Are you sure?" Even my mom, whom I told a week before surgery, asked if I was sure. That's a question many have asked me throughout my journey.

"Listen," I tell them, "For all of the folks who think trans and nonbinary people are having surgeries on a whim, they have no idea how much pain it entails, how much you have to prepare, and how much you have to put your body through to heal successfully and recover."

I told people that it was my body, that I knew what I needed and felt, that what I did with my body was my business and nobody else's. Having top surgery was literally one of the best things I've ever done for myself. I've felt grateful every day of my life since then that I'm finally comfortable in my own body.

Everyone in my life was ultimately supportive of me. But I was caught off guard, after my surgery, when they asked me if they should start referring to me with he/him pronouns. That was one of the furthest things from my mind because I was trying to focus on healing. I was ecstatic that I didn't have boobs anymore and could just finally be me; I forgot the entire premise of my gender identity.

When they asked me if they should refer to me with 'he/him,' I said, "okay, sure," since that's what I felt I should have been born as. However, about three months into everyone calling me "he," I felt this fear of no longer fitting into the lesbian community, which I had fought so hard to be a part of. I thought, *Did I just lose a place of belonging that took me decades to fit into, a place that helped me embrace my identity and love myself?*

Having this internalized conflict made me wonder, *Why do I have to pick one or the other? Why can't I embrace all facets of my identity?* Through evolution and growth, I've embraced all sides of the gender spectrum. My philosophy is that people aren't only one thing or the other. We're all a mix of many things and we shouldn't limit how we identify or feel most authentically ourselves. It was through that questioning that I came to identify as gender nonbinary with trans-masculine presentation. I know for sure I was born in the wrong body, but I've grown genuinely happy with just being me, a person who embraces both masculine and feminine energies.

As I attended more classes and talked to more educators and folks in the community, we all realized that the language will keep evolving and for every person, words mean different things. It can be very confusing.

Many wonder, "What is 'gender fluid?' What is 'gender queer?' What is 'nonbinary?' What's the difference between 'pansexual' versus 'bisexual?'"

As our society becomes more informed, new language develops because somebody will say, "Well, that doesn't fit me," and then another word or phrase comes into existence.

I started to publicly come out as gender non-conforming or nonbinary trans-masculine, and in the process, I started educating people (both queer and straight) about new terminology. There were constant questions and assumptions about terms like 'gender identity' and 'gender expression.' Those terms are not always associated with sexual orientation. I was frequently misgendered and miscategorized. Educating others about my gender expression and identity became part of how I introduce myself. And although I don't believe it is my obligation or duty to educate others, I have chosen to do so for those trans and gender non-conforming folks who can't have their voices heard or don't have the capacity to educate. Hopefully, by my educating others, they will pay it forward and pass that knowledge onto people they know, spreading awareness, not just about trans and nonbinary people, but about the complexities of gender. I believe understanding and knowledge will help bring an end to discrimination and hate.

BECOMING AN ENTREPRENEUR

For a time, I was working at my dream company, Google. I was a Senior Producer and it was fantastic, but as my time with them continued, there were many shifts in the company and I didn't feel like I was living up to my fullest potential.

After three years at Google, with several reorgs and then later an offer to move to another department or find a new role, I concluded that I needed to take a break. It was time to fulfill some of my other dreams, like starting a gender-free brand. I had been a workaholic for the previous 20 years, never took a vacation or traveled, and I thought this would be a good opportunity to take time for myself. So, I did.

I was very fortunate to have access to great health insurance at Google so, before I left, I took full advantage of my benefits and scheduled all the appointments I needed in order to complete my top surgery and hysterectomy. Once I recovered, I traveled to Europe and visited over 12 cities, the likes of which I had only seen in photos or studied in art history class. I was crossing off things on my bucket list, including watching a symphony in an opera house.

When I was planning the trip, I thought that if I was going to Europe, I would have to do one very important thing while there: learn about shoemaking. I was tired of not being able

The Real Lives of Transgender and Nonbinary Humans

to find comfortable shoes in my size, that actually fit my style and my identity. Being a multitasker and always efficient, I went on vacation, but I also decided to learn everything I could about shoe manufacturing, the shoe industry, and how I could start my own footwear company. Before I left for Europe, I established my corporation and filed all the paperwork because I felt called to solve this problem of footwear with gendered sizing and styles.

In Europe, I went to international shoe fairs and asked companies from around the world, "Why don't you make shoes that span across sizes that aren't specifically women's or men's shoes? Why can't you make men's shoes smaller so that women can wear them?"

Essentially, I was trying to explain how to make their shoes gender-free.

Unfortunately, because this is a predominantly old cis male industry, the reply was, "Oh, you want to make men's shoes in women sizes."

At first I thought, *Well okay, let's start from that point and I'll explain further*, but then the response became, "Oh, we know that there's a niche for this, but it's not worth it." They were saying that I'm not worth it, that my people aren't worth it. At that moment, I realized I couldn't only start my own company but that I MUST also start designing. I had thought maybe I could convince someone already in the shoe industry to fill this need but when I was told me and people like me weren't "worth it," I was determined to do something about it myself. If other companies, and the shoe industry in general, weren't going to create gender-free shoes that cater to people of all sizes and gender identities, then it was up to me.

TRANS AND NONBINARY
PEOPLE NOT ONLY
EXIST AND ARE
BEAUTIFUL, BUT
WE ARE MADE OF
COURAGE, SPIRIT,
INGENUITY AND
PERSEVERANCE.

When I got back from Europe, I pooled my resources and put together a Kickstarter campaign to publicly launch my company, NiK Kacy Footwear, and raised funds to begin production of the designs I had created using my savings. I told all my friends and promoted the Kickstarter campaign in the queer community. Even my ex-coworkers at Google were supportive of my campaign! It was my family that had the hardest time with this news. Because to them, an Asian family, it didn't make sense to leave your dream job and risk everything to start a company making something nobody else would. I understood where they were coming from but I still moved forward with my decision. When I believe in something, I don't just talk about doing it, I go out and I make it a reality.

My mom ended up being supportive, as were two other family members: my aunt and my stepfather. My stepfather was a lot more open-minded about the idea of starting my own business, as he told me he'd also started his own business when he was young. Unfortunately, his had failed so he didn't know if it was a good decision for me, but he still supported me. My aunt was extremely supportive. She lived in Memphis, so we mostly connected over the phone. I'd be sitting in LA traffic and talking to her every day on my way home from work. I talked to her about how everything was going and she'd tell me that she had many ideas for shoes and wanted to help me design, even though she was going through chemo at the time. It felt like our chats were the only thing motivating her and keeping her spirit up.

FAMILY AND LOSS

During this crucial period of getting my business going, I decided to travel to Memphis to help care for my aunt. It felt like becoming an entrepreneur was a gift from the universe that let me travel and do what I needed to do. Getting to spend time with her during her last few months is something I will always cherish. Unfortunately, shortly after my aunt passed, my dad made a wrong turn, fell down the stairs, and was paralyzed. A few months later, he also passed. When he was in the hospital, I had to ask myself, *Do I give this up so that I can take care of him, or do I stay committed to my business?* It was right before my Kickstarter began and I needed to be fully committed because crowdfunding campaigns are intense.

I realized, in that moment, that I'm not the kind of person to let go of one thing just so I can do another. It was stressful, it was hard, it was horrendous on my mental and physical health, but I was able to both care for my father and work on my business. The experience taught me that I can do anything if I put my mind to it. At the end of the day, I was glad that I made the time to be with my dad. I was able to help take care of him, support my mom in her most difficult time, and also continue with my dreams. He had been such an important part of my earlier years and he took such good care of me, my mom, and my family. Even though I gave him a hard time when I was a child, he earned the title of being my dad by the time I was in college and matured enough to realize he had already been my dad all these years. He was there for me and supported me when I needed it, and at the end of his life, I was there for him.

About a year after that, my dog of 18 years also passed, and it felt like my world ended. They say, bad things come in threes, but losing my dog was one of the darkest moments in my life. After being together almost every day for 18 years, the being who loved me unconditionally, who consoled me when I lost my aunt and my dad, was gone. The one who

The Real Lives of Transgender and Nonbinary Humans

slept by my side when I was recovering from surgeries or when I was sick or heartbroken was gone. She had been the one constant in my life, longer than any other living being had been, with exception for my mom. She spent more time with me than my mom did. When I was in a series of car accidents and was barely functioning with a bad back, it was adopting her that brought me back to life. After she passed, it was the first time since I moved to LA for college that I was truly alone and feeling hopeless again.

TAKING T

Being alone and mourning three deaths of beings I loved so deeply was extremely difficult, all the while still working hard to build my business and be a visible and proud figure for my community. I decided to start taking testosterone because, for the first time, I really didn't have anyone or anything I needed to worry about besides myself (since my mom didn't live with me). I never went on it before because I didn't want it to affect my dog. Dogs can sense these hormonal changes and I didn't think it was right to change my hormones when she was so old. I didn't want to stress her out.

When I did start finally taking T, I started with very small amounts to see how my body would react. I was worried about com-pletely passing as a man. I did not want male privilege since I fundamentally disagree with this inequality. It was something I felt very torn about then and continue to, still to this day. On one hand, I appreciate the physical body changes, but on the other, I don't appreciate the sudden privileges afforded to me just because I sound or look like a man. In 2020, after spending the ten months mostly in quarantine and surviving COVID (twice!), I decided to continue my course of low dose T in order to maintain a steady transition, without ever passing as a man. I do not want the privileges of being a man until there is gender equality. It just doesn't feel right to me, as someone who has experienced so much discrimination as an AFAB person.

MY CREATIONS AND GIFTS

The time leading up to the start of my company and the first year of operation were extremely challenging times, but I persevered. My first collection was more masculine-of-center. It's a bit more dapper than you would find in traditional foot-wear outlets. In addition to that collection, I had accessories, like leather cuffs and key chains, for people whose presentation is more masculine-of-center.

My second collection was gender neutral. I designed footwear and accessories that broke through the mold of traditional masculinity and femininity. I wanted the collection to make people ask, "Is that a man's or a woman's shoe?" and the whole point was that it's both and neither at the same time. I wanted people to ask questions and realize that shoes don't have to be gendered. Everybody can wear any type of shoe or clothing and decide for themselves how they identify with it. My mission was to break through binary gender stereotypes and help people understand that gender is just a societal construct. My goal as a designer is to help everyone express themselves authentically without society telling them they have to fit in this or that box.

For me, everything came together when I put the shoes that I designed on my own feet for the first time. It felt surreal. I had carried this dream with me for a long time. Everything that I'd been wanting came together in that moment, seeing my dream come to life, not just for me but for many others as well. My dream wasn't to design my own shoes per se. It was to finally walk in shoes that fit my feet and my identity.

Since I started my company, it has been mostly a one-person show. I am the CEO and the creative director, the designer, the website admin, the graphic designer, the photographer, the content creator, the salesperson, the shipper, and the customer service agent. However, along this journey, I've had the incredible support of so many talented and generous people in the community who have given their time, their skills, and their encouragement. The road hasn't been easy and I've given up a lot to pursue this dream. It's been a long journey—about eight years now—but I will say, for all of the blood, sweat, and tears, it's been worth it. I'm walking a path that's starting to become a lot more inclusive. I'm doing something I love and giving back to a community I love even more. Regardless of the struggles that I've faced along the way, I continue to walk this path because it is what feeds my soul.

Part of my community contribution has been starting Equality Fashion Week. I've wanted to give back in some way and, being in the fashion industry, I realized there wasn't a fashion week dedicated to the LGBTQ+ community. I created EFW for several reasons. Not only as a way to showcase queer designers from all over the world, but also to promote other small LGBTQ+-owned businesses; not only so our community can get the recognition and visibility we need and deserve, but also to provide economic development as a whole.

In 2018, we held the event on the rooftop of a boutique hotel in West Hollywood. 250 audience members attended, with about 80 models and performers; a pretty good turnout for a first year. In 2019, we moved to the historic Globe Theater in downtown LA, and had 750 attendees, with over 150 queer performers, models, and talent onstage. It's unfortunate that in our third and fourth years, we've had to cancel the live event due to the COVID-19 pandemic. However, I'm hopeful we may be able to do a virtual event to bring the community back together and celebrate our unity, safely.

One of my long-term goals is to spread Equality Fashion Week across the US and, eventually, the globe. In many cities where there are queer communities, LGBTQ+ people do not have access to queer fashion or fashion that helps them express themselves. Many designers traveled from all over the US to be part of my show in LA, which can cost a lot of money. Bringing the show to them not only allows them to showcase their work but also provides a platform for local queer talent and visibility to the local queer community and beyond. It also allows local people who aren't queer to see who their community includes.

THIS IS ME

If there's one thing that I hope you take away from reading my story, it's that trans and nonbinary people not only exist and are beautiful, but that we are made of courage, spirit, ingenuity and perseverance. Gender doesn't need to be this rigid construct, male and female with no middle ground. We play with our gender constantly in what we wear, how we talk, behave, act, and in most everything we do. From taking out the trash to cooking in the kitchen, gender stereotypes have constantly evolved throughout history. I educate people, whether they are friends, family, or even random strangers, through conversation, public events, and even fashion designs to normalize trans and nonbinary identities. We exist and we matter. We may face different struggles in our lives, but at the end of the day, we're people, just like you.

California law allows you to choose F, M, or X as your gender marker on state-issued IDs. When I went to the Department of Motor Vehicles to change my gender marker on my license to X, I had a really inspiring experience with the woman at the counter who was helping me. I went up and told her what I was there for, and after I spoke, she awkwardly looked like she wanted to ask me a question but stopped out of discomfort.

I made eye contact and gently told her, "You can ask me anything."

She told me that she had never done this before. She had never changed a person's gender marker to X and none of her colleagues knew how to do it correctly. She also said she didn't know what the X meant and she didn't understand why I was doing it. So I explained it to her. By the end of our hour-long conversation, she thanked me for explaining something so personal and profound. She was afraid to ask because she didn't want to offend me. I was glad that she did because hopefully by our conversation, the next person who comes to apply will have a much easier experience because their existence will have been normalized.

This is what I try to do every day: normalize the experiences that I and other nonbinary and trans people have, to get people not to make assumptions about a person's gender, lived experience, or identity. I wish that being nonbinary didn't affect my life the way it does, but we live in a very gendered world. Every time I want to pee, the gendered bathrooms come into play. I don't fit in the men's or women's bathroom because I don't pass as either or I pass as both, so this becomes an awkward situation. *Which do I choose this time?* There are some places that now have gender-neutral bathrooms which is great, but they're not always on the same floor or next to the others, which is inconvenient and marginalizing.

Managing gendered expectations is a constant day-to-day struggle, whether I like it or not. It's the simplest thing, something most people take for granted, but it can have a profound effect on how I am treated in any given scenario, something as simple as a car ride.

As far as we've come as a community and as a movement, there is still more work to be done and more voices to be heard, especially through mainstream outlets. Even though now there is much more inclusive content in entertainment and media, you still see representation not reflective of our experiences.

We're a multicultural, multigenerational, diverse community. We're not just trans or queer or gay or lesbian or nonbinary. We have many more layers to who we are, so our worldview and our experiences vary vastly. There aren't enough stories being told or shown through mainstream media that capture that diversity. I think the closest I've seen is probably at Outfest, a queer film festival held every year. Here you see a lot more accurate representation of queer folks and people of color. I want to see more of these stories told on bigger platforms, to larger audiences.

Part of my hope in telling my story is to fill that gap of diverse stories that need to be told. Speaking as a Chinese immigrant and a nonbinary trans person, I've faced numerous challenges and obstacles throughout my life, especially in my early years. I think that the universal experience for most queer people and people of color is that we have been forced to consistently overcome challenges. We are born into a society where we have to continually overcome adversity to get anywhere, so it's groomed me into a person who understands struggle. I have the perseverance of someone who has overcome and been challenged; now

The Real Lives of Transgender and Nonbinary Humans

I have the compassion and understanding for others who struggle and the faith of someone who's overcome challenges and continues to not only live, but thrive. All that has made me a better human, more compassionate to all people, whether they're strangers or people I hold close.

That experience has also made me a better business person, because everything that I create, everything that I design and produce, is made with mindfulness about how I want to help others overcome their own struggles. I want to share as much as I can and inspire as much as I can because I didn't have guidance or role models growing up. It's important for young people facing struggle to see somebody like them who has overcome those same or similar struggles. If they can be inspired and learn from my experience, I can make their lives a little bit easier than mine was.

As I continue to tell my story and give back to my community, I'm still growing and evolving every day. Sometimes I feel like I'll never be done transitioning. I'll always be growing in some way, whether as a business owner or just as a human being. I made the decision to live and I continue honoring that by living my life fully and authentically, making every choice and every action count.

I have people who love me. I have a great family and friends. I have a strong community and a house to live in. I may not be as financially stable as I had hoped to by this age, but my life is just beginning, and that's all the hope that I need. I have plenty of love to give and I hope to continue learning more each day.

I never really stop to think about everything that has led up to now except when I have moments like this where I tell my story. I've only shared the part about choosing life a few times publicly, and every time I share it, the reaction is so positive. The people listening are really glad I made that decision because of everything I've done since.

For any trans and nonbinary people reading this, don't be afraid to be yourself, whatever that means to you. Don't let anyone's opinions affect you or change who you are, just be who you want to be. Because at the end of the day, what I learned is that as long as you're genuinely, authentically yourself, the people who love you are the people who deserve you. The people who appreciate your authenticity are the people you should keep in your life. Never give up on yourself. Even if you feel like no one else believes in you, you have to develop that belief for yourself because only you get to live your life. Be proud of yourself. We all have the opportunity to make the most of our lives, to make the most of everything that we have, even if we have so little. It's really about the journey, and how you choose to live your life. Consider what you want your legacy to be, what you want to leave behind. We all have the chance to make a difference for ourselves and hopefully, for others too along the way. As my company tagline says, "walk your way."

Nik Kacy

DENISE BOWKER

> **Dee Bowker** (she/her) has a philosophy: "Being trans-gender is one of the least interesting things about me." She got her first job right out of college with an aerospace firm in New Jersey, but soon moved west and has been working with the same financial institution in Chicago since 1987. Dee has told her story both privately and publicly on many different platforms. She continues to share her story so that others will better understand why she transitioned; perhaps they will see some aspect of their story in hers. Dee's message: "You're not alone and you don't have to hide who you are. You can express yourself openly and authentically."

ISOLATION

When I was about four, I asked my mother, "Was a mistake made? Was I supposed to be a girl?"

I didn't know how else to phrase it at the time. When you're four years old, you don't have language to describe much of anything, let alone feelings about your gender. We talked about it for a little while, Mom trying to understand what I meant and me trying to explain how I felt.

At the end, she told me, "No, you are a boy. Go out and play."

My mom feels badly that, at the time, she didn't take me seriously, but I've told her that I understand; it was 1966, and neither of us were going to have the answers because back then, they simply didn't exist. If it had been 2016, the conversation might have gone differently. Language has evolved a lot in the past 50 years, but back then, the most common words to describe someone like me were unflattering: 'transvestite,' 'queer' (a derogatory term back then), and other offensive terms that wouldn't have helped my mom and me anyway.

Many trans people feel like they are trapped in the wrong body, but I never did. I never felt trapped as a guy, I just felt that it was wrong and that I should have been a girl. There are expectations placed on all of us when we're kids, and we generally make those expectations our own. That's what happened to me. I was dealt a specific hand in life and I didn't see a way to exchange my cards. As a kid, this led to me suppressing feelings during the day and to dreaming during the night.

Wanting to transition felt, at first, more like a desire than a need. I tried to manage as best as I could throughout the decades, but living with this unshakeable sadness became more and more difficult. Eventually the sadness turned into anger and the anger began to rule my life.

If you've ever tried to keep a secret from someone, even for a short amount of time, you know it can be exhausting. It's draining, always trying to make sure that people don't uncover your secret and doing everything you can to make sure you don't let it slip out. It's burdensome to do that for a week or a month, let alone for 50 years of your life. And if keeping a secret from one person is hard, imagine keeping it from everyone.

During the last two or three years prior to taking steps towards transitioning, little things would happen that pushed me towards the decision. I would be walking down the street, passing somebody who's got my build and around my age, and I would think, *I could be that person, I could be her. I should be her.* I remember once I thought, *God dammit, I wish I was her.* I was jealous of about half the population and I thought each time I felt the jealousy that there wasn't much I could do about it. Going through the same thoughts and feelings, over and over again, weighed on me. It was in those years that the drive to become my authentic self switched from a desire to a need.

For the majority of my life, transitioning has felt like a want, an ideal locked in the back of my head. I had gotten married and had two children, and thought navigating my identity with a family would be impossible. How could I come out to them and explain things while trying to keep the family together?

COMING OUT: THE BEGINNING

I never thought it was possible, but eventually it became unbearable to keep my secret. By this time, my kids were out of the house and soon to be married, which made things slightly easier for me looking back, but I still hadn't put all the puzzle pieces together.

In late 2015, I was in New Jersey for a high school reunion and staying with my sister while I was there. She and I were pretty close and I decided to confide in her about my gender. She did some research while I was at the reunion and when I came back, she had found a quiz online, ten questions that indicated gender dysphoria. I took the test and was like yes, yes, yes, no, yes, yes...*Holy crap,* I thought, *this almost fits me to a T!* There was only one box that I didn't check: the one that said, "I feel trapped in the wrong body."

My sister was, and still is, very supportive of me and she is my conscience. She is the person I confide in and ask for advice. From that initial moment, she has been one of my biggest allies and has helped me navigate my transition successfully. We talk all the time and she's given me some very good advice.

Every phone call, she would say, "You know, nobody cares outside of your immediate family."

What she meant was that nobody on the street or in my day-to-day life is going to care or notice that I'm trans. It took a few years to really believe it, but eventually I came around. Since then, I've added this piece: "If they do care, then they're a nobody." Why does it matter what other people think of me and my transition if it doesn't affect them, especially if they don't know me? My sister would drill that into me and after a while it sunk in and I realized yeah, a lot of people do care but they shouldn't, and I shouldn't let other people's judgements interfere with how I go about my life.

The second piece of advice my sister gave me was that there would be awesome days mixed in with terrible days. The good days will feel like a warm blanket, cozy and right, but then there will be days that are crappy, cold, and miserable.

"So when you have a really good day," she said, "I want you to remember those feelings and put them in an internal bank. Remember those times, what made you feel good, and how you felt so when a bad day comes, you can draw on those. Check out the good feelings like books from the library."

I call it 'banking the good days.' I've been able to get through some bad days through reliving wonderful memories.

About two weeks after confiding in my sister and starting to figure out this part of myself, I was crying a lot.

One day, my wife came home concerned and asked, "Who kicked the dog? What happened?"

I knew that I was going to tell her everything. It wasn't that I was scared to do it, I was more scared about the words I was going to use. I was cautious and wanted to be deliberate about what I was going to say since we were the couple that did everything together, we were happy, and we were looking at retirement together.

Throughout the years, my wife had always known that there was a feminine side to me, though she'd always asked me to keep it buried. We had been together for 30-something years at that point, and when I told her everything she took the news surprisingly well, on the outside. Over the next few months she came to understand the inner turmoil I was feeling. She agreed that there wasn't a choice in the matter, that transitioning was something I had to do. She was supportive, in the sense that someone can say supportive words but wasn't sure what to do to show that support. She's doing the best she can and I appreciate what she has done and continues to do for me.

TAKING THOSE FIRST STEPS

By the end of January of 2016, I figured I knew about half of everything about what the trans experience would be for me, what the path would look like for me personally, and what I needed to do in order to transition medically. I was going to therapy at the time and my therapist helped me piece together a lot of important information. She gave me resources about what trans people might go through and what I might experience. She told me to read the book, *She's Not There: A Life in Two Genders*, by Jennifer Finney Boylan, which details Jennifer's life and transition. I mentioned the book to my sister, who told me to put stickies on pages with passages that resonated with me. By the time I finished the book, it looked twice as big as it was because there were stickies on almost every page (some pages with multiple stickies) up to the point in the story when the author started to transition. I hadn't reached that point in my life, so I couldn't personally relate to anything later in the book, but it did give me good insight into what the experience would be like. She wrote about the emotional highs and lows associated with coming out and reaching transition goals, what it's like to finally feel comfortable with who you are and who you see when you walk past a mirror.

The other resource my therapist suggested was a 2003 movie called *Normal*, about a factory worker at a tractor plant in central Illinois who transitioned. I told my sister about it and she ended up finding it online and watching it by herself. She then told me under no circumstances was I allowed to watch this alone because she felt some of the scenes would be extremely triggering. There is one scene in the movie where the person who is transitioning is in a barn with a shotgun in their mouth, about to pull the trigger.

The Real Lives of Transgender and Nonbinary Humans

THAT IS WHY I
CONTINUE TO SPEAK
AND SHARE MY
STORY: **I DON'T WANT
OTHERS TO FEEL
THEY HAVE TO HIDE.**

These were the kind of scenes my sister warned me about, and when I saw them, I had to pause the movie and walk away to calm down. It was extremely powerful. My therapist wanted me to watch that movie to be aware of how intense transition can be and to be ready. I think my therapist was right; the social aspects of transition would have been more jarring had I not watched that movie and had I not been emotionally prepared for the possibilities of what lay ahead.

In addition to going to therapy, I started interacting with the trans community in different ways. One of the first things that I did was join an online forum for trans and gender non-conforming people. I was very active in the forums and later on I ended up meeting a lot of people from there in person. I met up with a few people in Florida, Pennsylvania, Illinois. I even flew down to Bogota, Colombia, with one of the moderators of the forum to meet with another person from the forum. While in Bogota, a few other trans friends joined us and the group grew to five. I have a framed picture of all of us together on my hutch cabinet and I cherish the memories of our weekend every time I see the photo.

Participating in that forum helped me tremendously. It gave me a place to go to post questions and get answers as well as read what other people were thinking and asking. People would post the same questions that I had, and I realized we all needed the same information. That's why, when people ask me questions now, I'm always happy to answer. I'm an AMA (ask me anything) kind of person.

Something else I did to get more involved in the community was join a Euchre game I found while searching for LGBT clubs in Chicago. Euchre is a card game that's popular in the Midwest. Two nights a week after work, I would drive the ten miles from my office to the bar where we would play. At first, I went in male street clothes with my old male name on the name tag. As the weeks passed, I slowly transitioned into female clothes and after a while, I realized that they thought I was just cross dressing. So the next time I went, I put "Dee" on my name tag, because I knew it was time to be myself. This was my opportunity to see how I would be accepted as being trans.

The club members' only reaction was to accept me completely and fondly. As my transition continued, the members grew closer and we've since become good friends. This was my first experience of being Denise and it went better than I expected. I was treated kindly and with respect. Overall the experience was very positive and reassured me that everything was going to be okay.

At the same time all this was going on, a local LGBT center in Chicago launched a new group for trans females (male to female). The founder, another trans woman, started the group in the first week of February of 2016 and I went to almost every meeting. We'd have about 15 to 20 people attending, many of whom were in the same position I was in. Most of us were just starting to understand ourselves and trying to figure out where and how to go forward. Through all the connections and support we were building, we became good friends and continue helping others that come into the group to this day.

I knew that part of moving forward with my transition was telling my kids. We always had a good relationship when they were growing up and that continued as they grew older.

Coming out to my son was an experience I'll never forget. At the time, he lived in New York City but worked for a company in Chicago. On occasion, he would come back to the area for business and we'd get together for lunch and catch up. So I invited him out to lunch one day, with the intent to come out to him. I had an elevator pitch I used to come out to people. It's not complicated or long; in 30 seconds, it's done and the conversation can continue.

While we were waiting for lunch to be served, I gave him the spiel. After I told him everything, I think he was taken aback; he seemed like he didn't know how to respond and ultimately, it was a short conversation. He changed the subject quickly, talking about how work was going and he clearly didn't want to go deeper or ask any questions. Since that initial moment, we haven't talked about it much.

The last time I asked him, his response was something like, "It is what it is."

His lack of—I don't want to say 'interest,' maybe 'curiosity' is a better term—didn't surprise me too much. He and I could talk about a lot of things. But he always went to his mom for "those types of conversations." I also came to realize that typically people who identify as male are just not inquisitive about this type of thing. It was a rare occurrence that conversations with guys about being trans lasted more than a minute or two. Coming out to those who identify as female was typically a 30 to 60-minute conversation.

Telling my daughter, on the other hand, was a different story. All in all, I've made very few "mistakes" during transition, moments where I regretted something I did. One was not coming out to my daughter myself. Her mom was going to visit her in Cleveland, a few days after I had come out to my son and at the time I felt it made sense for my wife to tell her. Now I realize that this decision meant I could never get that moment for myself, that moment of knowing what her true reaction was. The first second after you tell someone is the moment they show you their one true unedited, unscripted, honest response. After that first second, they've had time to process it.

I should have taken a day off from work and driven out there to tell her myself. I've had multiple conversations with her one-on-one, or with her husband who is usually there with her, but I've always wondered if she is really okay with this. Her reaction every time has always been yes, but when I ask if she has any questions, she doesn't have any. She's not the inquisitive type but it does make me worry. Although it's good to hear she is okay, I often wonder what questions she might have for me and what she's thinking about that she's not saying.

Everyone who transitions has a number of decisions to make. One of them is what to have your kids and spouses call you. One of the specialists that I've been seeing is my electrologist. Her dad is also transgender and when she talks about her, she always refers to her as 'dad.' We have talked quite a bit about it and the reasoning made some sense to me. I'll never replace my children's mother, nor do I want to. I'm their dad and at my request that's what they call me. Their spouses call me 'Denise' or 'Dee,' also at my request. When and if grandkids come along, I'd like them to call me 'Gramma Dee.'

After my kids and my sister, that left only my brother and parents to tell. My brother and I lived in the same town, about a mile apart. We didn't see each other very often, as he and I were never close and had different interests. I knew I needed to tell him, but I thought I would wait awhile, until one day I read that the local town council was voting the next day on a LGBT non-discrimination measure for the town. My brother was on the city council and if he voted against it, he would face future scrutiny within the family and the town, if/when people put two and two together. So I called him at work and asked if he could come over that evening because I had something I really needed to talk to him about.

That evening, we sat in the living room and I told him that I was transgender and that I was making changes that he should know about prior to voting. We did talk about the measure for a while but mostly it was about my plans and what other people's reactions had been. He asked about my plans for telling our parents but as with other guys, he didn't seem all that interested in the personal feelings I had or the "why."

As it turns out, the motion passed 8-0, with one abstention—not because they were against it, but because that councilor thought the bill wasn't enforceable.

That left only my parents on the list of people I absolutely needed to tell in person. So I flew to Florida for a long weekend. I arrived before dinner, and after the normal pleasantries and the meal, we settled down in the living room and I told them.

I think they were a little surprised and they didn't understand at first. We talked for quite a while and I brought up the time when I was about four and asked Mom if a mistake had been made. I think she felt guilty when I came out to them for not following up on my question five decades earlier. I assured her there was nothing to feel badly about. I have a great family, with two wonderful kids who I wouldn't have had the immense pleasure of raising had things gone differently. Besides, in 1966 when I asked, there were no resources and there was almost nothing she could have done.

My dad's comment was, "I don't see it, but it's not for me to see."

We talked about available resources he could use to educate himself. He stayed up late that night and printed out website after website, and in the end, he agreed with my assessment. Each website had one or two additional bits of information to add. Ultimately, he understood my transition and they both promised me their support.

My parents were 85 years old at the time, and they picked up on the pronoun changes very well. They make occasional mistakes but that's to be expected. How can I expect them to get it right all the time when even I make mistakes with my own pronouns? The one mistake that makes me smile is when they introduce me to their friends.

They'll say something like, "This is our daughter, Denise. He's from Chicago."

Now that they live in a retirement community, many of the people they're introducing me to are hard of hearing, and typically have a hard time hearing the "s" sound; I just assume they miss the "she" and hear "he" by mistake. But I find it sweet that they are trying so hard and doing very well.

While all this coming out was going on, I had already started my medical transition, with Hormone Replacement Therapy (HRT). When I first started to medically transition in March of 2016, there was an immediate and positive effect on my mental state. Three days after I started, I felt like a new person. However, as good as I felt mentally, the social pressure from those around me was starting to build. In late June, I came out to a married couple we had planned a trip with and they were considering cancelling. I could also tell that my wife was struggling with my transition when she suggested we'd need to sell the house.

The pressure from outside was more than I could stand. I stopped taking the hormones after three months and tried to put my relationships back together. This was extremely painful, to make progress, moving myself in the direction that I'd been thinking about for decades, only to then slide backwards.

Three months after stopping HRT, I was impossible to live with. I was quick to anger, always grumpy, and now looking back, I think undiagnosed depression was setting in. In late September, I became suicidal. I was with a friend who had struggled with substance abuse and they saw all the signs of someone who didn't want to go on. For the next four hours, they didn't leave my side. I will forever be grateful for their kindness that day and because of them, I'm here writing about my challenges and successes. Today, I am thankful to be alive, and every day is a bonus day for me.

On the following Monday, I called my doctor. We agreed on a dosage plan, and I restarted HRT. I haven't looked back since.

I've told this story to a lot of transgender friends, who've had similar experiences. Stopping HRT was like giving them a loaded gun. Transition has interesting effects on all aspects of a person's life, things I never expected like sleep. I would go without sleep for two nights, just lying awake on the bed, mind racing, unable to turn it off. Then on the third night, I would be exhausted and pass out. The next two nights, again I wouldn't sleep because of the personal turmoil I was experiencing. And on the third night, I'd reach a critical point of exhaustion where I would finally pass out again. I'd repeat the cycle for about two months. I was lucky that my wife stayed with me through all this and helped me break out of that cycle.

The next step was to tell my friends and the people I worked with. I knew I needed a simple way to break it to people without using words like, 'choice,' 'decided,' or other words that would imply that this was optional. This is the basic starting point for the next 100ish people I came out to:

Me: "Have you ever heard of 'Gender Dysphoria?'"

Them: "Uh, no." (Only two people had.)

Me: "Well, it's the clinical diagnosis for people who are transgender."

Them: "Um, okay."

Then I would allow a slight pause to let it sink in.

Me: "I've been diagnosed with it."

The idea was to let them draw their own conclusion that I'm transgender. I never said it directly but what I did tell them is that I was diagnosed and I was taking steps to feel better. The general reaction was acceptance and understanding. Some people were inquisitive while others were seemingly disinterested.

As I started to gain more confidence in how I was presenting myself, I knew I needed to take the final step and come out at work. I started in the aerospace industry right out of college and worked there for three years before moving to the Chicago area. I've been in the technology department of the same company, a financial institution, since 1987.

Since I've been with them so long, I transitioned on the job. I started transitioning in the beginning of 2016. By the beginning of 2017, things were starting to be pretty obvious. Whether to come out as gay, lesbian, or any other sexual orientation is a personal choice. You don't wear a sign around your neck, unless you want to, that says "I'm gay." For the trans community, once you start to transition, you have started a clock. In 10 to 12 months, everyone is going to start guessing and gossiping that something is going on.

There were two sides of my transition at work: the personal side and the business side. The business side of transitioning was interesting. I had talked to HR and my team about what I was going to do, so they knew before it was announced company-wide. I work on a team of six people, so there weren't a lot of people I had to come out to before it came out publicly two months later.

All throughout 2016, I started telling some work friends. In the beginning, I picked out five people, all female identifying, in five different areas of the bank to come out to. Them being in different departments was not intentional, it was just good luck. Using the same elevator speech that I used on my non-work friends, I would tell them my story. Over the next few months, I would have lunch with one of them each week, mostly to keep them informed, and they were curious. It wasn't until many months later that I realized that these five work friends were surrogate therapists. I would tell them what was going on and they would ask questions constantly. What I didn't realize was it was very convenient when things became public. I had five people who knew the full story, who were supportive and active allies, and who were in each area of the bank. When things went public, they would be able to answer questions that people didn't want to directly ask me.

The Real Lives of Transgender and Nonbinary Humans

I work in a company of 8,000 employees in Chicago, so there were a lot of people who had questions or concerns about me. Those five friends were my backup, my buffer, and they did an awesome job. They have been my advocates and allies since day one and they have made my transition at work all the more seamless. They watched me as I went through transition and they've had my back ever since. Whether they actually stopped any rumors or answered a lot of questions, I'll never know. Just knowing that they were well informed allies and could keep an eye/ear out for me made transition at work less stressful.

When everything finally went public in February 2017, I got a bunch of congratulations, and comments like, "You're so brave," and everyone was happy for me. It was great to hear and to know that my company was supportive. I also got an email from a partner in our Tempe, Arizona office. They had reached out to me because the news had reached them. They were the manager for the only other out trans person at the bank at the time. Apparently, there had not been another person who transitioned or came out on the job within the past ten years. The manager asked permission to send my contact information to Sandra, which is how we met.

Sandy became a mentor to me and guided me through a lot of what to expect and what I should do as I continued to transition on the job. I was extremely grateful for her. Her help and guidance later led me to be a mentor and a resource for others in the same position I was at the time.

One piece of advice she gave me the day before I showed up at work as Denise was "it will be the biggest non-event of your life."

She was right. I am unaware of any issues that occurred the first day or any day since.

People say that timing is everything, and my timing with respect to meeting Sandy was very fortuitous. She was scheduled to retire four months after I came out, which gave us four months to get to know each other. Sandy had created a "Trans 101" presentation through our company's LGBT affinity group and we decided that I would continue the tradition. The affinity group loved the idea of us doing the presentation as a tag-team before she retired. It was very successful, especially because she and I have different presentation strengths. I have since changed the presentation to fit my own style and have delivered it a few dozen times to other groups in Chicago, New Jersey, and London.

Everything was going well in my transition process, but towards the end of 2017, my wife had reached the point where she wanted to split up. The kids were grown and there wasn't a reason for us to stay together anymore. It wasn't what she had signed up for and she didn't want to be married to another woman. I accepted her decision and a few months later we were divorced. It was uncontested and we just split everything right down the middle. All and all, it was a peaceful breakup. We're still on good terms and there were never any bad feelings between the two of us. We still do things like Thanksgiving and Christmas together. We care for each other and want the best for one another. We just couldn't be together anymore as a couple, and that's okay. We're still friends and having her in my life in such a supportive way means the world to me.

MOVING FORWARD

The next step in my transition concerned the question of surgeries: which, if any, was I going to have, and when? When I first started this journey, I didn't know if I wanted gender confirmation surgery (GCS). Before I got to know more people in the community, I thought that everybody did it and that it was something that all trans people aspired to; that is not the case. There isn't a guide, like *Transitioning For Dummies*, so I didn't know that many people actually choose not to have surgery for a number of reasons. I kept an imaginary barometer in my head that measured the likelihood of me getting GCS. It started off at around 5 percent. I took some time to picture the surgery, to imagine what I would feel, and the barometer went up to 10 percent. A year later, it was up to 20 percent. At this rate, I figured I would either never have it or that it was a decade away. Then I saw the movie *A Fantastic Woman*.

I saw it at a small old theater on the north side of Chicago with a large group of trans friends. When we walked out afterward, the others were talking about how good the movie was and were all in good spirits, except me. There were couches and a bar in the theater's lobby. I found a secluded corner with a couch and I just sat there and cried my eyes out. I don't even know what I was feeling; probably the best way to describe it would be numb. The movie had spoken to my core and my soul. I was beside myself with a flood of emotions. I don't even know which emotions they were. It was overpowering.

Eventually my friends found me and wouldn't leave me. We were supposed to just go home after the movie but as friends do, they didn't want me to be by myself. We all went down the street and got pizza and they stayed with me for several hours until I considered myself coherent enough to take the train home. I was doing much better and everyone was super nice by texting me constantly, both that night and even the next morning. That's what friends are for and I have some of the best friends.

I remember exactly what scene in the movie affected me so deeply. If you've ever seen the movie or plan on seeing it, the scene that affected me the most was the one in the locker room. I remember thinking very clearly, *I will never walk into a men's locker room; cut this thing off now.* I was, at that moment, so sure that I must have "the surgery." My barometer went from about 20 percent to 200 percent; I remember thinking, *GCS needs to happen tomorrow!* I never wanted to feel like that again. That Monday, I called the surgeon I had been in contact with, and we scheduled surgery for about nine months later, on December 20, 2017.

The locker room scene in *A Fantastic Woman* was one of the most impactful on my transition. It's only ten seconds long, but it was powerful and watching it was a defining moment in my transition.

Just about every person I told that I was having surgery would ask me something along the lines of, "Are you scared, nervous, excited?"

I'd always say, "I am none of the above, this is just the next stage in the process."

That's also what I was telling myself. As the day approached, I'd get calls from the surgeon's office, and every time I got a call, my heart would stop. I would think, *Something is wrong.*

They're going to cancel, there will be some paperwork or something that will mean having to reschedule.

One day the call did come in, the one I dreaded and expected: one of the calls to reschedule. But lucky for me, they moved it up a week from the 20th to the 13th. The surgeon wasn't sure what the staffing coverage would be like through Christmas, so they wanted to move the surgery up a week early. That type of rescheduling was okay by me.

The day before surgery, I got a call from the hospital instructing me to show up at this time and what to bring and what to expect. Once I hung up the phone, every single emotion came out all at once and I could not stop crying. What I realized later was that I was feeling disbelief that everything was finally over. All of my issues about identity were going to be gone. Everything was finally going to be the way it always should have been. It wasn't an act of bravery or courage, this was just what I needed to be my true self.

SPEAKING UP FOR OTHERS

It's taken me decades to reach the point I'm at now. I've shared, and continue to share, my story across many different platforms. I've told parts of my story on stages, on podcasts, and now in a book. I've also spoken publicly. I have posted some videos on YouTube about what it means to be trans and the process of transitioning.

Through all of this, I've told my story to different parts of my company multiple times. I start at the beginning and by the time I reach the end, I've had people experience the full range of emotions, from crying to cheering to coming up to me and saying, "Thank you. I now understand my father."

The first time I gave a talk at my company, somebody in the audience hung around for a while until everyone had left and came up to me, saying, "Thank you very much, I'm next in line."

This meant they were next in line to come out to the bank and be themselves. Seeing me speak gave them hope.

That is why I continue to speak and share my story: I don't want others to feel they have to hide. I started to transition before I had knowingly met my first trans person and I don't want others to face that same challenge. I had no one to turn to and no resources that would help me figure this all out. It was terrifying not to have any first- or secondhand knowledge of what it was to be trans. I want to let people know that we exist and that I am that resource or go-to person I wish I had known before I first started. I can only imagine the positive impact on my life had I known someone who was trans back then.

I also want to help others be allies to trans people. Being an ally to any group—trans people, racial minorities, sexual orientation, etc.—is to be active in spreading positive and truthful information. Ally is a verb, not a noun. To be an ally means to take action and make change.

Having transitioned over the last five years, I've learned a lot about myself and people in general. There is an old prayer that I have taken to heart, "Lord grant me the serenity to accept the things I cannot change; Courage to change the things I can; and Wisdom to know the difference."

You cannot change someone's opinion and attitudes without changing their understanding. I live by that every day. I do not try to convince people that being trans is okay, that we should be accepted, or that we are normal people. I just be myself. I try to show people I'm just like them in many ways.

Most of my transitioning is complete at this point. I am who I am; accept me for who I am or don't. On two different occasions I've had new acquaintances tell me that their opinion of the transgender community has been turned on it's head because of me. After a bit of questioning, I learned in both cases they had negative feelings towards the trans community. But since they have gotten to know me, their understanding of what it is to be trans has changed for the better.

When I speak to a public audience, typically between 20 and 100 people, I emphasize that being trans isn't a choice. The choice was to transition or to not exist. Nobody chooses to be transgender, the same way nobody chooses to be left-handed. People should not have to go through each day struggling with themselves, with their job, with their friends and loved ones, and with the pain that they endure simply because of who they are. Especially when there is a way to make things better.

The emotional and physical changes are more intense than I had anticipated, but again, it was either this or not being here at all. My hope is that in being outspoken and con-veying these points when I talk and write, I'm able to point someone in the right direction, shed some light on what it means to be trans, and show them that they are not alone.

I don't regret the path that I've taken to get to where I am now. All of my choices have led me to where I am, right this minute. I have two of the greatest kids, I've got an ex-wife that I'm still friends with, I've got a good job, and my looming retirement is going to be okay. Life is good. I am my own person now. I'm not hiding and I can fully show who I was always meant to be.

For you trans or nonbinary readers, I'm going to give you the same advice that my sister drilled into me and that I've expanded: "Nobody cares, and if they do, they are nobody. Remember, there will be good times and there will be bad times, so draw on the good memories when you need them. Your life is your own; how you choose to go about things is up to you. But your life is not a dress rehearsal, it's the live show. There are no retakes. You are never alone."

Denise Bowker

TONY FERRAIOLO

Tony Ferraiolo (he/him) is an advocate for transgender and nonbinary youth and a Certified Life Coach. Tony shares his experiences to educate others and has started multiple support groups in his area for trans and nonbinary youth and their families. He is a singer, songwriter, artist, and the author of the books *Artistic Expressions of Transgender Youth*, Vol 1 and 2. These books showcase how transgender youth think about themselves and the world around them through their art. Tony is also the co-founder of the Jim Collins Foundation, a foundation that funds gender-affirming surgeries for transgender people. Knowing firsthand the lifesaving effects of top surgery, Tony co-founded the foundation to make sure that trans people in need have access to these necessary surgeries.

A PAINFUL PAST

At a young age, when I was about five or so, I didn't know the words to describe what I was feeling.

It's funny, because when I started hanging out with other trans people and hearing their stories, everybody says,

"Well, I remember when I was about five" and I'm going to say the same thing.

When I was about five, I was outside playing football with my brother, who's a year and a half older than me. He took his shirt off, so I took my shirt off. My mother screamed at me to come into the house. She told me that only boys take their shirts off outside.

I said, "I am a boy."

I remember her saying, "You're not a boy," and being very upset with me.

I thought she was lying. For years, I always thought people were lying to me and I never felt comfortable. Come Christmastime, I'd always be disappointed because I didn't want the doll, I wanted the truck. But my parents didn't know that. They had no way of knowing that.

Then puberty hit. I remember getting my first period and sobbing because I knew that this wasn't who I was and I didn't want this change to happen to my body. There was something deep inside me that knew I was a boy but I didn't have a way to express it in a way that other people could understand how I felt and help me with all the pain this was causing me.

Growing up, there were some times where a person would mistake me as a boy and say to my parents that they had sons and I loved that, but my parents would quickly correct them. I absolutely loved it when people would mistake me as a boy! But in school, it led to me getting bullied constantly. That led me to isolation and I really didn't have a lot of friends growing up. I was bullied so much that I ended up becoming the bully. I really tortured some kids as a way of dealing with my own pain.

In school I wasn't thinking about work or learning. I'd be thinking about the fact that I didn't want to go home. I grew up in an abusive household and a neighbor was sexually abusing me. I was extremely fearful and sad about the things I was going through in my house, which translated into anger.

There were times where I would come home and my father would be in a bad mood over something and would say, "Go to your room for three months," and he wasn't kidding.

Even though that sucked, the verbal abuse that I had to deal with every day was more painful. This was on top of being bullied constantly during school. Everything built up inside me and to deal with it all, I lashed out, putting all of my anger, fear, and sadness into hurting other kids and hurting myself by turning to self-harm.

There was one time when I was in my early teens, probably 13, that my father threw me out of the house—typical behavior for him—and I was on the back porch with my dog Pepper. Pepper was my protector, who would keep me company every time my father threw me out of the house. It was getting dark and I was getting scared because I hated the dark and where we lived, there were a lot of bats. My mother eventually opened up the sliding glass door but when I went to get up, she called the dog in and shut the door. That, for me, was one of my darkest days. How could my own mother call in the dog and leave me outside?

I do think back to those days sometimes, thinking about what I said and did to some of those kids and it's very upsetting. I was a kid that was struggling but that's not an excuse for lashing out at others. There were, and are, healthier ways to deal with what I was going through, but now being on the other side of everything that happened, I think that all the moments that I've gone through, good and bad, have created the person that I am today.

I also think about my dad, hearing all the stories that I learned about him growing up and what his upbringing was like. There were moments (not a lot but occasionally) where I'd see him clench his fist and cock it back but restrain himself from following through with it. I think about what my dad must've gone through in his house and the reasons why he didn't follow through with that fist.

All the abuse was finally too much for me to handle, so one day I went out to buy a pack of cigarettes and I just didn't go back. I couldn't keep going back to the abuse, again and again, day after day—it was too much. Now homeless, I didn't have an immediate place to go or someone to rely on. That was the first time that I had to go to the bathroom outside. I didn't feel human, I felt reduced to something less than, that this was what my life had led up to. Thankfully, I was able to couch surf for a while and I was only homeless for about a month until I found a place that I could stay.

YOU CREATE YOURSELF

As I got older, I fell into drugs. I was dealing and using coke and pot, just to get away and escape from the reality that I was in. I was still cutting myself. For me, it was a way to survive all the pain and torment that I was still going through. A way to keep going, you know, keep living. Trying to fit in where I could, but also wanting to escape from it all, so isolation was my friend.

For years, I didn't know who I was and I never had a strong sense of my identity. I started to identify as a lesbian, because I was attracted to women and people were telling me I was female. There were no words for who I really was and I only took on the label of 'lesbian' because of what other people had been telling me. I didn't feel comfortable at all with the way my body was and the way that other people saw me. I didn't have sex with my clothes off. I made sure that I wore boxers and a tee shirt all the time. I didn't allow anybody to touch me. I didn't hug anyone because, with my breasts, it was emotionally damaging. Think about it, hugging someone was emotionally damaging. So I always kept people at a distance and I constantly felt like there was something wrong with me.

I was a club promoter and I used to throw these huge dance parties, where there would be 200 to 300 women there. Everybody would be having a great time. They would leave laughing and happy, and I would go home and cry. I would snort coke, drink, and smoke pot because I felt like a freak and needed to numb that pain. Outside of throwing those parties, I was pretty much depressed every day. I remember almost every night, sitting on my couch wondering if I really wanted to live the next day.

How did I survive? I started a lesbian band called Vertical Smile. There were three of us, and we played local gigs. One night, the lead singer Jean and her wife Elizabeth came over to my apartment with a bag full of videotapes saying tonight was "trans night." I'm sitting in my chair thinking *What is she talking about? Trans night?* But she knew my struggle and knew that deep down, I needed to watch these films.

She knew about my struggles growing up and that part of that was because of my facial hair. People would tease me all the time, over and over again because of it.

SOMETHING HAPPENED:
SOMETHING INSIDE
OF ME SCREAMED,
"CREATE YOURSELF,
CREATE YOURSELF!"

One day I was talking with Jean and she said, "You know, we should go away some time for the weekend and just let it grow out. We'll see how it looks."

When she said that I was like, "Oh my god, that would be so fucking awesome."

She didn't look at me like I was a freak, she thought that what everyone else was teasing me about was a cool thing. What a boost to my self-esteem!

So, when she came over for trans night, we watched the *Gendernauts* documentary. There was a trans guy on a beach and he pulled open his shirt and said that he'd had his surgery. When he did that I literally almost passed out and I was like, "Oh my god, I'm trans!"

I remember being really excited about it, knowing that everything kind of made sense now. The way I've always felt and the way I couldn't connect with my body, the emotional gut punch I would feel in my stomach whenever I heard the terms 'ladies,' 'she,' or 'woman' applied to me. Everything that I had been feeling was finally starting to come together and make sense. I was so excited about discovering this. Jean and Elizabeth knew that I needed to know this and they were happy that I finally came to realize who I was.

I remember Jean looking at me and saying, "Just be...Just be Tony."

That moment of recognition and understanding was cut short though when I stopped thinking about the past and started thinking what this meant for my future. I didn't know any trans people and, unfortunately, the only stories I had heard about trans people were either about trans women getting murdered or were quick punch lines. *How do they survive? How am I going to survive this?* I couldn't imagine being trans and being happy or successful or even having friends. I was so unhappy as a lesbian, who the fuck would accept me as a trans guy?

The thought of living the rest of my life scared and unhappy left me hopeless, so I went to the beach to end my life. I remember sitting on a park bench, crying so much I could barely see the water. You see, I didn't want to die, but I thought I didn't have a choice.

Then something happened: something inside of me screamed, "Create yourself, create yourself!"

I remember thinking, *Wait, I can create myself, I have all the power to do that.*

I started to think about what Tony would look like. I imagined Tony to be this really cool, artsy, tattooed guy with a goatee. But then I went a little deeper, *What would Tony's emotional state be like?* You see, I didn't want to be angry anymore, I didn't want to carry around the weight of all the pain that I held from all the abuse in my life. I wanted so badly to feel inner peace. I wanted others to smile when they were in my energy. Just thinking about the person I could become brought a feeling over me that is hard to explain. It felt warm, it felt right, and it certainly felt like a feeling I could get used to.

A STEP FORWARD

It was the end of 2004, and not only was top surgery my number one priority, it was the only thing I thought about and talked about. I lost some friends because they were just tired of hearing about what they thought was an obsession.

Remember, I didn't know any transgender people when I transitioned, and my friends were the only people I felt safe talking to about this. So I started to do the research. I found a doctor and made the appointment for March 9, 2005.

I knew I needed to "get my house in order" and it was important to tell my employer. I was so scared, because I didn't know if I was going to lose my job. In 2005, over 90 percent of transgender people who were transitioning on the job were losing those jobs.

As a manufacturing manager of a small business, I led a team of about 35 people. I had no idea how people were going to react to this. I went to the VP who handled HR and let her know that I was going to take time off because I was getting surgery.

"Are you ok?" she asked.

"I will be," I answered. "I'm getting gender affirming chest surgery; I'm transitioning."

Her reaction was very respectful, and she went on to treat this like she would any other type of surgery. I was grateful, but still worried about losing my job once I came back to work. Nobody was talking about transitioning openly. That's what made this so difficult. I told her that when I came back to work after my surgery, I would be using the pronouns he/him/his.

The funny part for me was that she wasn't surprised and neither was anybody else I told. I always had a very masculine gender expression, so much so that when I was telling people that I was going to transition they were like, "Oh yeah okay, that makes sense," and nobody was remotely shocked.

Thankfully, there were no issues at my job, and the surgery went off without a hitch. Having all that weight off my chest (literally!), it felt like my life truly began at that point. The moment I looked into the mirror after my chest surgery and saw the person I've been wanting to see my entire life—that changed my life and led me down the path of helping change other people's lives.

When I came back to my job after recovering from surgery, the owner and president of the company came into my office and said, "'He' now, right?"

I said "yes sir, 'he' now."

He said that he would make sure that everybody knew and not to worry about it. I was so thankful for him accepting me and welcoming me back. If I wasn't accepted and welcomed back, I am not sure where my path would have led me. Luckily, I didn't have to spend this newfound energy for life on worrying about my livelihood.

Not everyone had made a seamless transition to accepting the version of me who came back to work. There were a few people that were having a hard time because of their religion.

But the biggest issue when I returned to work was that nobody told me what bathroom to use. Being a manufacturing manager, my office was right in the manufacturing area where there's two bathrooms: male and female. I didn't feel comfortable going into the male bathroom, where there were going to be all these guys and I didn't know how they felt about me. Even though I have led them for years, I didn't want to create these awkward tense moments. And going into the female bathroom would have made that ten times worse.

In the front office, there were also two gendered bathrooms. They were single stall bathrooms, but I still didn't feel comfortable using either one of them. For the first two weeks, I went back to work part-time, since I was weak from all the blood I lost during surgery. I worked from 10 a.m. to 2 p.m. When I was part time, it wasn't bad. I would just make sure I went to the bathroom before I left my house and I would hold it until I went home. Then I went full-time and still nobody told me what bathrooms to use. I would leave work at lunch, drive a mile and a half down the road to a gas station, buy a bottle of water and a candy bar, and ask if I could use their bathroom.

After about three weeks of that, I was gaining weight because of the candy bars and I was like, "This is bullshit, I need to talk to someone about this."

So I went and talked with the VP about it and I told her that I had been using the gas station bathroom for the past three weeks.

"Well, just use the men's bathroom in the front office," she told me.

Still to this day, I use that bathroom. It's what I feel comfortable doing and it was almost like all I needed was assurance that using the single stall wasn't going to start an uproar in the plant.

This is something that I teach now, as a speaker talking in front of large audiences.

I tell them, "If you're in a public bathroom, and you see a person walk in and you're questioning their gender, I can guarantee that they are more afraid of being in that bathroom with you than you are of being in there with them. Get over it, wash your hands, and leave. They are only there to use the bathroom, and nothing else. We are terrified about what could possibly happen to us when we are in a public bathroom, the verbal or physical harassment that could happen to us for just trying to use the bathroom for the purpose it was built for."

There was a specific instance where I was talking in front of a school district, training 150 or so school professionals and administrators. And I said to them, "I'll tell you what, if you promise not to tell anybody, I'll let you in on what trans people do in the bathroom."

All of the people in that audience leaned in and I was like, "God, you guys are really leaning in? We pee! That's what we do in a bathroom! The only thing you should worry about is if we wash our hands after we're done! We are just there to use the bathroom like everyone else; there is no big secret, it is not a social event."

HEALING MYSELF AND OTHERS

During recovery from my top surgery, I had a follow-up appointment with my surgeon, where she would take off my bandages and I would see my chest for the first time. My heart was racing as I was called into the exam room, scared of what I was about to see. The surgeon came in and took off the bandages and I just sat there.

"Well, aren't you going to look in the mirror?" she asked as she pointed to a full-length mirror that was hung behind the exam room door.

Thoughts were running through my head...*What was my chest going to look like? Would this be enough for me to be happy with my body,* a body that felt like it didn't belong to me for so long. I walked up to the mirror with my head down, holding on to the surgeon's shoulder to brace myself. I took a deep breath and looked in the mirror.

I could not believe what I saw. For the first time in over thirty years, my mind and my body matched. Instantly, I stood up taller. I felt handsome, and happy. On the drive home, I thought *No one should ever miss out on feeling this way because they don't have the money to pay for this type of lifesaving surgery.* That's what led me to co-found the Jim Collins Foundation with Dru Levasseur a few years later. Through the foundation, we provide gender affirming surgery funding for trans people who need it, but do not have the ability to pay for it themselves.

After recovering from surgery, more and more people started asking me to talk to them about my experiences as a trans person. It was a complete reversal from when I transitioned in 2005. When I transitioned, there were very few people who were out in my community. Now all of a sudden, people started hearing about this trans guy.

Friends of friends of friends would say, "Hey, I got a friend who wants to transition, Can they meet you?" and I'd say, "yeah."

I used to meet people at Starbucks and it was almost like my office. I would start guiding people—very slowly and kindly—and empower them to walk their truth.

I started doing that for trans kids and their families and that led me to get my certification as a Life Coach. I'm now also a certified teacher of mindfulness meditation. The work that I was doing was growing. I started several support groups for trans youth and their parents. I was leading these groups, trying to help and inspire other trans people. All of this work is extremely rewarding, educating and helping others. But one of the hardest parts of doing this work is when I'm at a psych hospital, visiting a transgender or nonbinary youth who just doesn't want to live anymore.

What do you say to a child between nine and thirteen years old when they say they just don't want to live anymore? How do you empower them to walk their truth and help them feel that life is worth living?

When I am sitting with them, and they ask me, "Why should I live?" I tell them, with all the love in my heart and soul, "Well, I want you to live. I've been in that exact same chair that you're sitting in and I can help you. You're not alone."

A lot of times they tell me, with their head down, that I won't ever understand, that they are cutting themselves. I tell them a bit about my background and the struggles that I've gone through.

I look at them and I say, "I used to cut myself."

And they're like, "What?!"

I say, "Yeah, I used to cut and there's no shame around it. You're fucking surviving. Good for you! That's how I survived and that's how you're surviving."

I say to parents—and they hate when I say it in front of their kids, "There's nothing wrong with them cutting themselves. That's survival but I'm going to make sure that we can find a more creative way for them to express themself."

When I started creating, I stopped cutting. I take all that pain and put it on a canvas. My art and creativity involve a lot of very abstract stuff and found materials, like rusted barbed wire, bottle caps, and things like that. That's how

The Real Lives of Transgender and Nonbinary Humans

I'm able to channel the pain and emotions into something creative.

Through creating art, going to therapy, and having top surgery, things got a little better. When I started healing myself, I started to have kindness and empathy and compassion for myself. Everything started to change. I used to be a kid that was struggling, yes, but I don't feel like a victim anymore and I certainly feel separate from who I used to be. Now I feel like a survivor and a warrior.

In creating myself, I still had to work on my body dysphoria. Even though I had a male chest now, I knew bottom surgery was not for me. I didn't want it but I still had dysphoria around it.

One day, when I was seeing my therapist, David Tate, I was really struggling and he said, in a matter of fact way, "You have the body of a trans guy."

When he said that I was like, *Holy shit, he's right. I have the body of a trans guy. And if I want to change my body, I can.* This all came full circle when I was sitting with a young trans boy, who was very, very dysphoric; he was a cutter and a stitcher. So, not only did he cut, but he stitched at the same time.

I was talking with him and he said, "You don't understand. I'm trapped in the wrong body. I was born wrong."

I sat there thinking, *Even though I'd struggled with the same things, I didn't know what to say at that moment to comfort him.* I was still trying to put the pieces together in my own mind that we aren't born in the wrong bodies.

WE'RE STILL
OURSELVES, WE'RE
NOT TWO DIFFERENT
PEOPLE. THE ONLY
DIFFERENCE IS THAT
NOW WE CAN **RELAX
INTO OURSELVES AND
WE CAN GET WHAT
WE NEED** IN ORDER
TO BE OURSELVES.

I had gotten him to the point though where he didn't have a plan to commit suicide or hurt himself and I felt comfortable with him leaving the session. So when he left I sat in the silence. For me, in silence is where the answers are. You can't hear the answers if you're not silent.

All of a sudden it came to me. I realized that we're not born in the wrong bodies and we're certainly not trapped. We are born in our bodies. What's the biggest thing that riddles our community? Depression and anxiety.

So every time I'm training, I say to the cis people in the audience, "Let me ask you a question: If somebody told you that you were born wrong, would you be depressed? Or if someone told you that you were trapped in the wrong body, would you have anxiety?"

Imagine that being told to you, over and over again, over the course of years. It builds up on us, to the point where some feel that there is no other option but to end their life.

That's what I said to this young trans guy, the next time he told me that he was trapped and born wrong. I gently corrected him with a smile and said, "You were born in your body and if you need to change your body, I am here to help you." I asked him, "Do you need a binder?"

I've been doing binder drives for more than a decade and have probably given out about 500 binders, at no cost, to trans and nonbinary people around the world, young and old, who need them.

So we got him a binder and I said, "What else do you need?"

"Well, I'm getting my fucking periods."

I told him we can stop that too. So I talked to his parents and they were onboard. They brought him to the doctors and he got his Lupron (hormone blockers for children entering puberty) and he didn't get his periods anymore. Through that, we saved him because we were allowing him to express himself and be himself.

In doing this work, in listening to these kids' stories, their stories affirmed mine and I felt this deeper connection working with them. As much as I healed and helped them, they also healed and helped me. Working with these young trans kids is what led me to write and create my series *Artistic Expressions of Transgender Youth*. These are books that celebrate and showcase the creativity that young trans people have. Through their art, they are able to express how they feel and what they are going through internally in a physical form.

The books always have two questions; there's a really heavy question and then a lighter question. For volume two, those two questions are, "What makes you sad? And what do you want to be when you grow up?" In that I write about how anger is a fueled emotion. You can't just be angry. It comes from fear, sadness, or frustration.

Part of the reason why I am so deeply invested in what I do, is because of the first time I saw a human shift from a sense of hopelessness to hopefulness right in front of my eyes. That happened because of something that I said and that human just being in my energy. That was transformational for me. I'm able to be the person that I needed when I was struggling in the same way. If somebody was back there saying, "You're okay and it's going to be okay," I don't think I would have struggled as much. When you give someone hope for a better life, they won't want to take their life.

However, life comes at you in completely unexpected ways. When I told my family that I was trans, most of them cut me off from their lives. I went without talking to most of them for about seven years. What changed was that I had kidney cancer, twice. I was misdiagnosed the first time and was told that I would probably be alive for about five years. A week later they backtracked their diagnosis saying that they thought I just had an abscess. So a lot of emotional shit between those two diagnoses. I had stage one kidney cancer on my left side first and then they found it again on my right side a year and a half later.

I've been cancer free on one side for six years and on the other side for five years. But throughout the surgery and treatment, my thought was like, *This is it*. Cancer is a scary thing. Actually having it and living through it is even more terrifying.

My cancer brought my family members, who walked away when I transitioned, back into my life. I still keep in contact with them. We're not a close-knit family to begin with, but there are times where we come together as a family. One of the recent events was my parents 60th wedding anniversary. My whole family was there and we all got along better than we ever did. We're all older now and people just accept me for who I am. Everybody knows I'm a happy and kind person. It is awesome being accepted and loved, simply for being you.

In my work with trans youth, there have been multiple parents who freak out and don't know what to do when they find out their kid is trans. But once their kid is able to walk their truth, the transformation they see is incredible.
I had a father once say to me, "I drove home and I got out of my car and was like, 'what's that noise?'"

He said it was his daughter laughing. His daughter is a trans girl. He couldn't remember the last time she laughed, but that she started going to my groups and made friends.

He said, "I didn't recognize my own child's laughter."

When we're able to be ourselves, that's when we shine the brightest.

A BRIGHTER DAY

In doing all this work, I'm currently working on my third book. I plan on writing a memoir. There's been a documentary made about my life. I try to take a moment, every now and then, to reflect. Like how the hell did this happen? How was I able to come from that dark place that I grew up in and get to the point that I'm at now? Inspiring trans and nonbinary youth, educating others. I truly believe everything changed for me once I started to create myself.

I spoke at an event for Trans Day of Remembrance (TDOR), which I do every year. I brought everybody into a loving kindness meditation. Once we finish, we say the names of the trans people who were killed in the last year and remember their names; it's pretty triggering and emotional for people. I did a little speech before all of this and I talked about a realization that came to me a few weeks ago. I realized that when I talked about myself, I would always refer to my pre-transition self as another person.

A lot of people in the community don't want to think about the person that they used to be and I used to do the same. I referred to that person as her. She was the one who was strong. She was the one who survived all those suicidal thoughts. She was the one who survived all the abuse and allowed me to be Tony. I was separating myself, like my pre-transition self wasn't a part of me. I wasn't taking credit for the strength it took for me to get from that kid who was cutting themselves in the woods on a daily basis to who I am today. I wasn't taking credit for that and I realized that that person is a part of me, it's a part of my journey and what I've gone through.

We're still ourselves, we're not two different people. The only difference is that now we can relax into ourselves and we can get what we need in order to be ourselves. It's just that now we're getting what we need, just like anybody else who has something wrong with their body; they work to change it and now they're okay.

Out of the darkness of your past, you can walk into the light of your future. I'm not letting my history dictate my future. I might've been beaten, abused by others, and even abused myself but it created the person who I am today. I don't regret what has happened in my life. I'm now proud of who I am, I actually love myself for the first time ever. It's a good feeling, I find myself smiling now. When I'm able to get out of the trance of life, the go go go mentality of always being ready for the next thing, I try to sit in that moment and I can feel so much joy from my life. I can cry. That's how happy I am.

If there's one piece of advice that I can give to any trans or nonbinary person reading this, it's to walk your truth and surround yourself with people who love and honor you. I remember the first time I came out to my lesbian friends as trans: I was pretty popular back then and I was hanging out with a bunch of people.

A few of them said, "You're not trans. You're just a bull dyke."

I tried to explain that I am trans but when they rejected me again, I stopped hanging out with those people.

I remember going to dinner at a bar with my ex-girlfriend and another lesbian couple and I went to the bathroom.

When I came back out, I kind of stood back and looked at them, watching them talk and mingle with each other. I remember saying to myself, and really feeling it, that this was not bringing me anything. I wasn't gaining anything positive from these relationships. Life is not a dress rehearsal and your time shouldn't be spent with people who don't build you up.

The cruel reality of this, and our lives for that matter, is that some of us will lose our families. If you don't have a family to support you, create one that will! We're out here. You can create any family you want, but also create room for your family to walk back in. The majority of my family didn't talk to me for seven years after I transitioned. They were struggling. It's a shitty thing. I'm not saying that I agreed with it, I felt that they should have been able to struggle in their own way but not in a way that completely cut me off from them. So I always kept my heart and soul open to them and I knew that someday that they would walk back in.

We can't force people to accept us. It doesn't work that way. So for your own mental health, if you end up in the same position that I was in with my family, it's okay. It's better to accept the fact that they loved you at one time and they might come back. Don't stop your life over it. You can create another family. Just never let go of your light. You have to live as yourself, to live your truth because it is a life worth living. Somewhere down the road, you may be the one that's lighting someone else's torch.

Tony Ferraiolo

SAMANTHA LUX

Samantha Lux (she/her) is a transgender social media influencer, YouTube content creator, and speaker. Through her Samantha Lux YouTube channel and speaking engagements, she shares her journey with people across the world. Her goal is to educate those outside the trans community about what it means to be trans and about inclusion. She gives back to the trans community by being a voice for people who have never met a trans person, those questioning their gender identity, or are transitioning, as well as people interested in learning what it means to be an ally. She currently manages her business Samantha Productions, and is a full-time speaker for numerous businesses, events, and organizations across the world.

FITTING IN

I was born into a small-town family, with an older brother and sister. My brother was the epitome of masculinity. He did everything a stereotypical boy would do growing up and acted exactly like a typical older brother. I felt like I was living in his shadow. My sister, on the other hand, was gorgeous, the epitome of femininity. They were inverses of one another. While there was pressure and an expectation to follow in my brother's footsteps and be like him, I wanted to be more like my sister. I attempted to do the things she was doing and act how she was acting.

Growing up, I looked up to my sister as a role model for the things I hoped to one day be able to do. I was excited about the idea of putting my hair up in a ponytail or wearing dresses like the ones my sister wore. As a kid, I got away doing a lot of girly things. My mom was actually the person that I confided in the most about the things that I wanted to do.

Like if I wanted to paint my nails, I would wait until everybody was gone and I'd ask, "Can I borrow your nail polish really quick?" and she'd say, "Yeah, yeah, but you have to take it off before Dad gets home."

I did a lot of small things like that, which made me feel more girly and feminine. I would wear my mom's heels or I would take bandanas and tie them around my head, or over my waist, pretending that it was long hair or a skirt. There was even one Halloween I can remember, when I was supposed to be a ghost, but to me the bed sheet acted more like a long, pretty dress. So I would literally wear it every day, cause I felt cute and happy wearing something close to a dress. My cousin and I used to play princesses and put on jewelry and clothes. Most of the time the game was just 'be a princess,' no real game involved.

As I got older though, I started to learn what was socially acceptable and what wasn't. The boys made fun of me when I grew my hair out, so I learned that I had to keep it short to avoid being harassed. For a while, I stayed friends with the same girls from elementary school, but as we got older, they learned that it wasn't cool to hang out with the boys, and I lost them as friends. I tried to not be seen publicly as 'girly,' but it didn't matter—hanging with the boys, they picked up on it and called me 'gay' or 'girly' and other names. From that harassment, I learned that I had to hide how I was feeling inside. I understood that I could only express myself when I was alone or, at least, to be more discreet anyway. For instance, if I wanted to wear jewelry, I figured out I could wear 'boy jewelry' and get away with it being socially acceptable. At my house, with friends visiting, I made sure that there wasn't anything noticeably girly in my room. I was critical of the smallest hint that might give me away (like my American Idol pin) and would hide it away, wanting so badly to have friends.

Over time, I learned that I had to also keep things hidden away from my dad, who was very traditional.

He always made jokes like, "If you ever came out as gay, you wouldn't be able to stay here."

He made jokes like he never thought someone in his family would ever be LGBTQ+. While it was supposed to be a joke, it made me anxious and cautious about expressing my feminine side around him. My mom remained the person I confided in the most, talking through how I was feeling about things, but only to a point, since I wasn't even sure how to express how I felt.

Hiding myself weighed on me heavily enough that I started therapy for depression, anxiety, and eating disorders at an early age. Most of the time, I pushed down everything I felt in order to fit in, to belong and have friends. But that only made me hate my own image. I never liked my appearance.

When I developed an eating disorder around my freshman year of high school, the therapist asked me, "Can you find one thing about yourself that you like and we'll start there?"

I sat, blankly, for about 30 minutes. I had never found anything about myself that I liked. I actively avoided mirrors and if I did see myself, I couldn't stand to see who was looking back.

The hard part to explain to my therapist was that it wasn't me that was looking back. It was someone else trying to adjust, someone else suppressing all the feminine feelings so that people would accept me and be my friend. Deep down, I knew that wasn't me, but then I was left with the question: Who was it then, looking back at me? If I didn't feel comfortable in my own body, then there must've been some reason and something that I needed to figure out about myself. Through therapy and self-exploration, I settled on the idea that I was gay. It was a step in the right direction in figuring myself out.

The first thing I had to do was tell both of my parents. Given my mom had always been understanding, I figured (and hoped) she'd be supportive.

Sure enough, when I told her, she responded, "Is that it?"

My concern shifted to telling my dad. Given his former dis-criminating comments, my therapist and I decided I should write a letter, since he wasn't the best listener. A letter would mean he'd have no choice but to read it. It took him a few months to make time for it, but eventually, when he did, it was really awkward, especially in light of the remarks he'd made in jest about gay people, which he now knew applied to his own kid. The jokes stopped. In his way, he was trying to reconcile and figure out how to support his kid. It was another step in the right direction though, and I felt like one thing had at least been figured out.

Even at 17, I didn't really know-know what being trans was. When I was a kid, I remember feeling like, "Oh, I can't wait to grow up and do" this or that. I knew I wanted to do things like be able to put my hair in a ponytail, or wear dresses, or do feminine things. Later, I realized that I was never going to be able to do any of those things if I stayed the way I was. Being a girl still seemed impossible; it seemed like a wish that I could only make real in my dreams. Figuring out my sexuality was a step in the right direction, but I was still dealing with a great deal of gender dysphoria, without even realizing what that was or what it meant. I spent lots of time watching makeup and beauty videos on YouTube, living vicariously through other people like Gigi Gorgeous. Through them, I started to realize that the dreams and wishes that I longed for could be a reality. It allowed me to take a step back and say, "I can do that—I can actually be a girl." It can be more than a wish or dream. It could be real.

I dug deeper into what it meant to be trans, things like what hormones, gender dysphoria, and transition meant. The videos gave me more information about trans people, who were just living their lives like everyone else. It began to make me think that even though I'm trans, I'm just like everyone else. We're just people, living our own lives. It felt like an answer, like, *Oh, I know what I need to do now. I know the path that I'm supposed to be on.* In a way, it was instant. The moment I heard a trans person's story, everything that they said aligned with mine. All the feelings I had made sense. So much of my depression, anxiety, and eating disorder were amplified by my gender dysphoria. I was feeling so unhappy with my body and appearance and now I understood why. Now I felt like I could do something about it.

THE REALITY IS THAT
**I WILL CONTINUE TO
GROW AS A PERSON.**
EVEN IF THE CHANGES
ARE NOT RELATED TO
MEDICALLY OR SOCIALLY
TRANSITIONING, I WILL
ALWAYS BE GROWING
AND CHANGING, EACH
AND EVERY DAY
**BECOMING MORE OF MY
AUTHENTIC SELF.**

A JOURNEY SHARED AND REALIZED

If I was going to move forward with myself and my life, I needed to come out to both of my parents again. I guessed my mom's reaction would again be supportive, based on her reaction to me being gay.

When I talked to her about being trans, her initial reaction was, "Can't you just be gay?"

We had a long conversation afterward, where I explained how I was feeling, what this meant, and what I wanted and needed to do.

At the end, she said, "If this is who you are, then we'll figure it out. We'll get the best help and we'll do whatever we can to help you."

It was a huge win for me, having her support and knowing she would always be there for me, to make sure that I was happy.

One of the first steps I took was switching to a gender therapist to help me work through my gender dysphoria. It allowed me to learn what it meant to navigate the world as a trans woman. My biggest concern was coming out to my dad again. My mom kept my secret for a few months; we only talked about it when my dad wasn't around. She shared a genuine concern that his reaction could lead to the end of their marriage. She eventually opened up to him about me. He didn't really comprehend it, almost like he didn't believe being transgender was a real thing that people could be or that it could apply to his own kid. When faced with the truth, he denied it. He had to rewire his entire perception of trans people and reconcile it with who I was.

Before going off to college, I had a conversation with him and told him that I loved him and hoped he could be there for me.

I explained, "This is what I have to do now. This is who I am, and transition is the path that I have to take to be happy and move forward with my life."

In so many words, I asked him to choose. Either he was going to be there for me or I was not going to talk to him anymore.

At the end of the conversation, he was still struggling to come to terms with everything, but we said, 'I love you,' and ended the night. Over the next couple years, I could see he was trying to be supportive but that it was difficult for him, occasionally misgendering me here and there. The important part was that I could tell that he still loved me. After a while, when I started hormones and began living as my authentic self, he started to see how much happier I was. That's when he really got it and fully embraced me for who I am.

Before I went to college, I was still digging into all kinds of trans stories online. As great as the resources were, they were still obscure or few. If I hadn't clicked on one video that was pivotal for me, I don't know where I'd even be right now or if I'd still be trying to understand why I feel this way. There was a gap in representation about trans people, especially in mainstream media, which constantly used trans people as a gag like "she's secretly a man." It didn't seem like trans people were real, just something to poke fun at and a cruel punch line to get a cheap laugh from the audience.

I wanted to fill that gap, not necessarily trying to be the person that defines the trans experience, but to be a voice

The Real Lives of Transgender and Nonbinary Humans

like, "Hey, I'm trans and I'm not scary!" I also wanted to give back and be a role model for somebody else, so a trans person could find my videos and start to realize who they are. As a result, I started my own YouTube channel and documented my transition. Three months after I gained my mom's support, I started HRT and documented it on YouTube. A few weeks later, I started presenting to the world as 'Samantha' and that was the beginning of it. Every month or so, I would post a video giving an update on my progress and how things were going; I would tell a story about something that had happened to me that I thought might resonate with others. Eventually, as I started college and grew more through transition, so did my YouTube channel.

That didn't mean that all of the things that I was working through were magically fixed when I started college and HRT. About six months to a year after I started my transition, I began dating men and had heartbreak after heartbreak. I thought I loved them and that I'd be with them forever. When that didn't happen, I blamed being trans for causing my disappointment. I blamed not having surgery or, even after having surgeries, that I wasn't pretty enough or not doing this or that enough. I just always brought it back to the fact that I was trans. I had plenty of days when I couldn't leave my room because I was so upset about how nobody in the world would ever understand what it was like to be trans. There were days where I believed that other people called me a girl because that's what I wanted, but really, they would always see me as a boy. I feared they wouldn't ever get it on a deeper level and understand what it's like, day in and day out, to struggle so much with who they are.

The only kind of romantic attention I got after my transition was either from boys who didn't know that I was trans (who cussed me out and blocked me as soon as they found out) or from boys who did and only liked me *because I* was trans (and fetishized me). I had to strategize dating and tried everything: telling people immediately; telling people after a day; telling people after a month of talking—if I waited to tell them, they'd get mad because I didn't fit the image in their mind or live up to it. As if coming out to them as trans somehow shattered the image of who they'd been talking to, as if all they could see now was this thing, and not a girl or even a person. It took time for me to see it was on them and not something I was doing, especially when being trans was only part of my identity.

Things have gotten a bit better today, with more social awareness about trans people since my transition. People will still ask invasive questions, but at least they have a general idea of what being trans is. Even still, I feel the effects of having to always hide my identity and feel shame about who I am. Like with my current boyfriend, he'll touch my leg and I freeze up, triggered from past experiences.

Even though I put updates on my life and transition on YouTube, I was cautious about telling people I was trans. Online there's a degree of separation between me and a person just watching my video, compared to someone knowing and interacting with me in my personal life, especially when I'm trying to have a relationship with that person. A video is just a small snippet of my life that anyone can watch and take what they want from it. In person, I don't have the benefit of separation.

Dealing with my own dysphoria, coupled with feeling undesirable, I did everything I could to have the surgeries that I needed to feel good about myself. I was lucky to have supportive parents, who helped me get through the surgeries in a very short period of time. I would schedule them during semester breaks from college; Mom and I would travel together. Nine months after I began HRT, I had my first gender affirming surgery: removing my Adam's apple. My dad began to realize that this was a thing, and that I was going to need more surgeries, and it scared him. Not just because they were performing surgery on my throat, but also that my transition was becoming more real. But when he saw how much happier I was and that I was finally finding peace within myself, he started to come around and realize that transition was what I needed.

Four months later, when it was time for the first part of my bottom surgery (gender confirmation surgery, GCS), my dad was much more onboard. Soon, I had the second part done, where the doctors did the detailing work. It's more aesthetic, where they form the clitoral hood, the labrum, and clean up any visible scar tissue. It gave me peace of mind, knowing everything would be corrected, especially since there had been a complication during the first round of surgery. One of the sutures had ripped apart and the whole area was swollen: the only recourse was to let it heal on its own. In the follow-up, the doctors were able to remove the extra scarring and make things more aesthetically pleasing.

About three months after finishing my second bottom surgery, I had my top surgery. After each surgery, I felt more and more like myself. When I was finally done, it felt liberating. For so long, I never wanted to look at myself in the mirror and see who was staring back at me—I never wanted to be intimate with anybody before and it held me back from a lot of things. The closer that image in the mirror came to the image I had of myself in my head, the more comfortable I became in my own body, and the happier I was. Things finally felt right and I finally felt like myself. I could move forward with my life, be okay with who I am, and pursue the things that I wanted to pursue.

GROWING A BRAND AND GROWING AS A SPEAKER

I posted my first YouTube video a few months before I went off to college. Every couple of months, I would upload a new video giving an update or telling a story about something related to my transition. I was anxious and nervous about putting my story out there. I didn't know what the reactions would be. Knowing how social media can be, and the kinds of comments that people leave on the internet in general, I didn't know what people would say to someone transitioning. Would people be supportive of what I was putting out there or would there be a barrage of degrading comments filled with slurs?

Even though I was extremely anxious about posting my first video, I did it because I wanted to document things for myself and for others in the community. Going through the comments of those first videos, there was a wave of positivity and support. Sure, some of the comments were negative and hurt to read, but the number of positive comments far outweighed them.

Posting more videos and putting more of my story out there, I've gotten to the point where I just ignore those comments. They're not funny or original, and I can only be called a slur so many times. I've tried to respond to comments, I've tried to engage in a conversation and educate people, but I've come to understand they aren't looking to be educated. People who post hateful comments and negative things aren't going to change their minds and the same comments will be posted on the next video. It got to a point where I'd just block certain words so that I wouldn't see those hateful comments—as a rule, I ignore any negative comments on my videos.

As I was going through college and having my surgeries, I documented my recovery and progress. The more videos I posted, the more my channel started to pick up traffic. Little by little, I realized the power of having an audience and fan base, and the positivity that I could bring to people by sharing my story. I would read comments that people left, saying that before seeing my content, they didn't understand or know anything about trans people and now they know a little about what it's like.

Reading that my videos have raised awareness, that I've been a resource for people to learn about trans people, or that I've been able to help someone through their own transition is immensely rewarding. I've read comments from parents of trans kids, saying they didn't know how to support them before seeing my videos, and comments from trans people, saying that my videos gave them hope. These small random comments of positivity make me feel like, *Okay, yeah, putting myself out there and starting this was worth it.*

As my channel grew and I kept putting more of myself out there, my mom wanted to do the same and share her own story. She's always been a super great ally, always doing research and wanting to help. All of her effort paid off when she told a part of my story at her workplace. She was asked to speak about her experiences and educate some of her coworkers about what it means to be trans and a member of the LGBTQ+ community. Everyone was surprised when she made it known that I was there in the audience, listening to everything.

That was the start of us speaking together, sharing our stories and growing that into a speaking business. After that first time she spoke at her company, we were approached and asked to share our stories again through workshops her company was doing. Her workplace really liked what we did and it took off from there. People would recommend us and other companies would reach out to us, asking if we could do a presentation or workshop with some employees. If the company had a Pride event, they'd ask if we could come and share our experiences. If a company had an employee who was transitioning, they'd bring us in to make sure that they were doing everything that they needed to do to offer support, while also educating other employees.

We developed a routine of how we would go about conducting our speaking engagements. My mom talks for the first half, telling her story; she's really good at relating to people and pulling people in because most people have a mom. Most people can relate to her situation, especially as a parent. Then she'll talk about me, and I'll come up and do some trans educational background for the duration. Introduce them to someone who is trans and give the basics about what being trans is and what it means.

One opportunity begets another, allowing us to grow our business as speakers, supported by my original YouTube channel. I never expected or came close to thinking that by posting a few videos and putting my story out there, it could become so much more. It's real work and impacts the lives of so many people. I'm so grateful to have this opportunity and platform to share my story.

LOOKING BACK AND GIVING BACK TO THE COMMUNITY

Having gone through it all, including the surgeries, in hindsight, it's like a dream. I still deal with anxiety and depression, but now, I can confidently say that I do love my life. I never thought that I'd get to this point or even be able to transition in the first place. I remember when I was younger, I said to myself just about every single day, *I can't wait to grow up and be a girl.* For so long, I thought that it was never going to happen.

But it did! I'm far enough along in my transition now that I don't have to worry about every single move I make or about whether even the tiniest thing that I do could out me. When I first started my transition and started to live as myself, all the time, my friends would be like, "Oh you're so good at acting like a girl." They didn't mean it in a bad way, or understand how much it hurt; they just meant that I was passing really well. I told them that I didn't really do anything. I just stopped trying to be this person that I wasn't. I started living authentically as myself. Once I let loose, the rest came naturally to me.

When I first transitioned, it seemed like I was never going to be done. I know this was in part because I wanted to pass so badly and because of this perfectionist idea that I used to have about what passing meant. I was always moving toward something and I feel like that's still kind of true. After each surgery, I would switch to the next thing, like, *Okay, what else can I fix? What else needs work? What else can I do to help bring myself closer to the person that I want to be?* As a trans person, I felt like I had to constantly get everyone else's approval that I am a woman and that I am who I say

I am; it put a lot of pressure on me. The reality is that I will continue to grow as a person. Even if the changes are not related to medically or socially transitioning, I will always be growing and changing, each and every day becoming more of my authentic self.

That is something that I wish I could've expressed more when I was growing up. I wish I could tell my younger self that it's okay to like what I liked. All those years wasted, policing my own gender and restricting myself based on what other boys did and liked. I wish that I could go back and tell my younger self to stop trying so hard and do what I wanted. I would have been a lot happier, and I wouldn't have felt the pressure to check everything that I was doing and saying.

I do think that things happen for a reason though. I don't know how things would have been different if I had decided to be more authentic earlier, if I'd decided to take that first step and be who I was at a younger age. I don't think I'd be sharing my story in this way, having a YouTube channel, or even a speaking business. All the struggles that I've endured in my life have led me to be the person that I am today and continue to work on every day. But it's worth saying, you don't have to police yourself like I did. Take it from my past self, it's better to be happy with who you are, than to try and get people to like you for someone they think you are. The people who like you for who you are will stick with you and support you to the end.

I've shared my story in the hopes of providing inspiration to anyone who isn't sure that things get better. They do. I've taken after other trans YouTubers, like Gigi, and historical figures, like Marsha P. Johnson—those who risked everything to pave the way for future generations. I feel like, if they can put themselves out there and share their stories, then so can I.

It's my way of giving back to others who may not have the same opportunities that I have. I was, and am, extremely fortunate to have supportive parents who helped me get the things I needed, like the surgeries. I know that isn't the case for everyone.

I want to find the best way to use the privilege that I have to give back, uplift, and be a voice for the trans community. Whether it's educating someone about what it's like to go throughout the world as a trans person or giving hope to someone who's struggling with family and feeling like they'll never be able to be who they are, knowing that I've helped even one person makes everything worth it. Like with everything, taking that first step is the hardest part, but once you move forward in your journey to be more of your authentic self, it gets easier. Time heals all wounds.

One piece of advice that I will give to any trans or nonbinary person reading this is to do what you can to stay safe. Not everyone understands us as much as we'd hope they would. So I always tell people to be safe. It might seem like a given within our community, but I do think it's important to test the waters and be sure that someone is supportive before coming out fully, even with friends and family. This way you can get an idea how they will react when you do come out to them.

I also want to say that things do get better. Even though I was able to transition really quickly, when I was in the middle of it, it felt like I was never going to get to my end goal. It took time to reach this point in my life where I am happy with where I am. The hardest part is trying to make that safe environment for yourself. Carving out a piece of the world that's for you and filled with people who love you. It's hard, but it's doable and it's worth it.

The other piece of advice for those struggling, who can't come out to their family, is that your biological family isn't necessarily the family that you have to keep forever. If you're not safe around them, find a new family. At school, maybe you can find friends that make you feel safe and that you can be yourself around. Even if you're not living with them, at least you can express yourself, be authentic, and be safe.

As we get older, we can choose who we want to surround ourselves with, and over time, we grow our own communities and support systems. Often, it is our chosen families that provide us with the most support and what we need. You can always find other people and build your own family. You deserve to be surrounded by people who love and care for you.

The first steps are the hardest, but don't ever stop pushing your life in the direction that you want it to go. You will eventually be at the point in your life where things are good—they may not be now, but they will be.

Samantha Lux

GAVRIEL LEGYND

Gavriel Legynd (he/him) is the founder and CEO of Visioneer IT, a marketing and technology firm specializing in web development, social media marketing, and Cyber Security Solutions. His personal endeavors include supporting the LGBTI community—specifically, trans people—to be empowered and true to themselves. He is also the co-chair of the Transgender and Gender Non-Conforming Task Force mentorship committee for the National Gay and Lesbian Chamber of Commerce's (NGLCC), which offers coaching for trans business owners to become a certified LGBTI Business Enterprise. He also serves as the Vice President of the African American Marketing Association and sits on numerous boards. He is a father of four, grandfather of four, a Jew of color, and a proud vegan.

UNDERSTANDING MYSELF

As a child, there was a small, still voice that told me who I was to become. The language to describe what I felt was not fully developed, so it took the form of me being a slight rebel. On many occasions, when told to act "ladylike" I would insist that I was a boy. My mother quickly corrected me, but I was adamant.

"No, I'm a boy!"

Finally, she asked, "How do you know you're a boy?" and I told her, "Because boys pass gas!"

Kids my age always said girls don't pass gas, so I put it together, and thought, *If I pass gas, then I'm a boy.* She wasn't amused, reinforcing what everyone else kept telling me—"Hey, you know you're a girl, right?"

Resisting took the form of doing all the things that my older brother did. He was my idol. He is seven years my senior and I wanted to be just like him when I grew up. He was well liked, tall, played football, and he had what seemed to be a lot of girlfriends. Although we were so close growing up, little did we both know that, years later, he would decide to remove himself from my life.

I didn't grow up in a family that talked about gay or lesbian people, let alone trans people. In fact, the first time I heard the word 'lesbian' was in elementary school, when I had a crush on a girl. We were on the playground and I kept wanting to sit next to her in the play-castle. One of the kids called me out on it, and called me a lesbian. I didn't know what it meant, but I understood by the way the girl twisted up her face in disgust that it wasn't something good. In hindsight, 'lesbian' wasn't a word that fit me because I was a boy, and boys liked girls, so it seemed natural for me to be attracted to them.

PARENTHOOD AND COMING OUT

During high school, I had my first daughter at 16, and my second at 19. By eighteen, I was married to a man and my priorities shifted to that of a wife and mother. As a mother, I knew my daughters were my main priority, which left no room for me to explore the odd feelings I had growing up. Instead, I was busy figuring out how to put food on the table and keep a roof over our heads. Although I was a very young parent, I went on to college and eventually obtained my Ph.D. and several other graduate degrees. My marriage ended in divorce by the time I was 20 and it was then that I had my first lesbian experience.

Coming out as a lesbian was liberating. At the time, the word 'lesbian' felt right, but in hindsight it felt right only because I was not aware that there was another option. My first relationship with a woman felt right—or seemed to make sense, but I felt like there was still something missing and off about my identity. At least now I knew I was pairing myself with the right gender. While I still identified as a woman and dated women, the label of 'lesbian' placed on me didn't necessarily feel 100 percent right. Over the years, I gradually began presenting more and more masculinely. Eventually, I changed my appearance by cutting my hair and wearing only men's clothing. My girly sway was exchanged for a manly swag. I felt as if I was reclaiming my body and, for the first time, I was comfortable presenting as a butch lesbian, even though deep down I wanted everyone to address me with male pronouns.

By early 2000, I was starting to identify as a stud but internally I identified as a male. I wasn't heavily involved with the LGBT community, but I yearned to find other trans men with whom I could identify. Being based in the DC-area, I saw an overwhelming number of trans women. However, trans men were not visibly out—especially not trans men of color. After joining a few online groups, I met a woman whose daughter was dating a trans man who hadn't begun his medical transition yet. His name is Shane. He was also thinking about transitioning. Eventually we met, and it was through my friendship with Shane that I learned there was a possibility that I could transition too.

Shane and I talked a lot about transitioning, so much so that he suggested we go through it together to offer each other support—but I couldn't do it. I was scared. I had only recently learned what the word 'trans' meant. It felt like it was an all or nothing type thing. I didn't know that you could cherry-pick which parts of transition worked for you. Everything I read online made it seem as though everyone's transition entailed hormones and surgeries that could only take place in another country. It never dawned on me that I had the right to design my own transition path.

After spending some time doing more research on what transitioning would look like, I started digging deeper into how this choice would impact my life. My number one concern was losing my family, especially my kids. They were depending on me and I didn't want to lose any of them through my transition. The more Shane pressed for us to transition together, the more I reflected on my responsibilities as a parent.

In so many words, I told him, "Your life isn't necessarily my life," reminding him of the differences between us, like his being white and having no children.

I told him, "Being a white man in America is a lot easier than being a black man in America, you know?"

That was my truth and he understood.

He said, honestly, "You're right. I see you and I hear you. I understand that I'm not a black man. There's a lot more at stake for you."

From that point on, Shane stopped pushing for us to transition together, but we remain friends even to this day.

The years came and went but the idea of transitioning stayed with me, always in the background, wondering what it would be like, what would change physically, and what it would mean for my family. I watched from afar as Shane transitioned. His face changed, his body changed, and I could tell he was truly living his best life.

While the news touted stories about celebrity transitions, like Chaz Bono, there was not much in the way of visibility for trans men of color. What I realized is that the trans community was its own separate sphere from the lesbian and gay community. You had to know where to look and who to talk to in order to find a place to fit in.

My decision was made even more difficult based on my limited knowledge of medical transition, which was peppered with false information regarding hormones and cancer. It took me years to work through my own doubts. It finally reached a boiling point and I wound up talking about it with my then wife. I told her point-blank that I wanted to be treated like a guy and that I was trans. She didn't know much about what transitioning entailed. At the time, I wasn't sure either about how to transition and whether hormones would be part of it, but what I was sure of was that it was important to me that she treat me as a man. Although she was a bit perplexed by my choice, she honored my wishes.

GROWING TOGETHER AND SEPARATED

Six months into being married, I decided it was time. I officially told my wife and daughters only a couple of weeks before I took my first shot. I asked them not to worry, emphasizing that I was going to still be the same person. My oldest was supportive at first.

"You can be whatever you want to be, you know, that's fine with me," she said.

My youngest daughter cried and grew upset, saying that she didn't want to lose her mom. She was young and scared, and had no idea what to expect. None of us did. They had a ton of questions, to which I had very few answers. I was unable to help them understand simply by way of pointing to another family member or person who was in a similar position and say that this was how things would be. Looking back on this time period, I understand that the biggest reason why I had no one for my family to reference was in part because, historically, trans men were very stealth. They didn't want to be outed as being trans for a variety of reasons, but primarily due to safety.

I remember my first shot so vividly. A couple of days later, my voice changed and my energy level went through the roof. I didn't think anyone noticed the change in my voice until one morning a few weeks after my first shot. I went to my daughters' room and knocked on their door to say it was time to get up—only I didn't recognize the voice that came out of my mouth.

The Real Lives of Transgender and Nonbinary Humans

My oldest said, "Who's that?"

She opened the door and looked nervous, thinking a stranger was outside her door.

She said to me, "I know I was supportive, but I think you've gone too far."

She didn't expect such a radical change so soon and closed the door on me. It crushed my mood; I was so excited to hear my voice, but now I could see the effects that it was having on my oldest daughter. Before I started hormones, it was my youngest daughter who was most upset about the transition. But as it turned out, she ended up being my biggest supporter and appeared comfortable with the changes that I was going through.

The early days of my transition were documented with weekly pictures of my face and body and even a daily journal. My goal was to turn it all into a flip book so I could document my progress. I asked my daughters to write something for the book. Both of them did. My oldest daughter wrote, "It's so wonderful to have a mom like him." At first, I was a little disturbed by a 'mom like him,' and then I thought, *Well, she used the right pronouns!* It was okay. She knew I gave birth to her and that's what a mom was, even if now I happened to be a man. Me transitioning did not change the fact that I was their mom. The title of 'Mom' did not define me. Today my youngest daughter calls me 'Daddy' and my oldest calls me 'Cletus.' I'm not sure how she chose that name but it stuck and I still answer to it. We have all settled into a new normal in our relationship. Although publicly my daughters introduce me as their dad, they still come to me for motherly things too. I am so grateful I get to be both in the same lifetime.

WALKING LIKE A MAN

Being raised and socialized as a female was never some-thing I thought would impact how I related to people post-transition. I never thought I would have to consider that the way people would perceive and interact with me would change when presenting as a visible man. Not just from being a trans man but a *black* trans man. Nobody prepares you to be the stereotyped scary black man. Before transitioning, I remember being able to have conversations with women in elevators, just easy, casual conversation. Mentioning things like, "Oh, I like your purse," or "That's a nice perfume you're wearing." Then one day, those easy, familiar conversations were gone. I became aware that women now saw me as a threat. By becoming a man, I gave up the right to make comments to women in passing. I could no longer say to a woman, "Hey, I really like your style," without it being automatically assumed that I'm coming onto her or that I want something. Their body language told me that I was not to be trusted. I often wondered if it was my blackness or my maleness that scared them most. It made me feel disconnected and a little bit lonely. I wish there were more conversations being had with trans men of color to prepare them for how to be a man of color in America and what to expect.

Transitioning is not just a physical process, resulting in passing as a cisgender person, it is also spiritual and mental. Transitioning comes with a whole new set of responsibilities, expectations, and losses. Everything changed, down to my relationships, communication, how I thought, and even how I smelled. I had to relearn how to interact, with both men and women.

THE JOY THAT I HAVE
ISN'T TIED TO
RELATIONSHIPS OR
OTHERS' ACCEPTANCE
OF ME. **IT'S JUST TIED
TO MY RELATIONSHIP
WITH MYSELF AND
THE REALIZATION
THAT I *AM* ENOUGH**
AND I ALWAYS WILL BE.

JUSTICE ISN'T BLIND

My mother didn't take my transition so well. I can't think of anything that I wanted more than her acceptance. Having her support would have made me feel invincible, as if I could brave any trial that life dealt me. Our relationship hit a hurdle when my mom decided to take me to court for custody of my oldest daughter, who was expressing feelings of depression. Reflecting back on why my daughter acted out, I believe she was struggling with a multitude of things, including my transition. Losing custody of my daughter (the day before my birthday) was unbearable. It cut deeper than anything I had ever experienced. It was devastating to have the legal system demonize me because I had decided to transition. Me being on hormones and having surgery were brought up as reasons why my daughter should not be in my custody. They saw me as a stereotypical scary black man, who was putting my daughter in danger.

The judge told me, "You're a man and she's not comfortable with men."

I guessed this was the price I had to pay to live authentically. In the end, my daughter returned home once my mother realized that she was a handful. After returning home, my oldest told me that it wasn't my transition that was causing her defiance, but rather just her becoming a teenager. In hindsight, I could have done more to make sure my children were emotionally prepared for the choice I was making. After all that happened, it took time to repair and heal our relationship. Some things are still painful to talk about but what matters most is that we love each other.

The Real Lives of Transgender and Nonbinary Humans

COMING OUT PUBLICLY

Once I started passing, I decided to be stealth, not wanting to draw attention to myself. I kept it on a need-to-know basis but over time that became exhausting. I wasn't able to have meaningful conversations where I could bring my whole self to the table. Those people who I befriended never had the pleasure of really getting to know me. The life I created was a myriad of stories that would make me appear normal. I lied and created stories to fill in the gaps of who I was and what I was doing before transitioning. It was agonizing making up reminiscent locker room talk about football and sports I'd participated in during high school, knowing full well that I never played a sport in my life nor did I even watch sports on TV. But I wanted to fit in, by any means necessary, and fitting in by any means was exactly what I did.

At one point, after I had become an Ancient Free and Accepted Mason and risen to become a 32nd degree mason, I realized how tired I was of living a lie. After years of membership at my lodge, my fellow masonic brothers discovered that I was born female and I was asked to leave. Although it was another devastating loss for me, I knew it was necessary and that it was the only way for me to really grow into the man I wanted to become.

It wasn't just me who was tired of the lie but also my family. I would go to extensive lengths to prep my daughters if we were going on a family outing by telling them, "Don't slip up and call me 'mom.'" Or "don't do" this or that. It was one thing to worry about myself making a mistake, but a whole other thing to worry about my family slipping up and misgendering me. In short, I lived a double life.

CHAMBERS SOMETIMES SET YOU FREE

Weeks turned into months, months into years and before I knew it, a decade had passed. I was still stealth and I had started my own business. I had never really been a social person but now that my children were grown and I was an empty nester, I wanted to attend networking events to help grow my business. One day, I registered for an event that, unbeknownst to me, happened to be a matchmaking event sponsored by the Maryland LGBT Chamber of Commerce. I knew right away I had found my community. It was one of the first times after transitioning that I felt safe enough to even contemplate coming out.

The first time I said, "I'm trans," aloud to a group of the chamber's members was at one of their events. I was terrified about what they would say and what their reactions were going to be. I think they were all trying to figure out whether I was gay or just an ally. When I told them, one of them said something like, "we would've never known." Not only were they accepting but they ended up inviting me to be on the executive board. Being on the executive board provided me with many opportunities to allow myself to be seen. It resulted in me having numerous opportunities to share my story.

In a way, trans men are now where trans women were many years ago, in terms of visibility. Through my involvement with the Maryland LGBT Chamber of Commerce as well as the National Gay and Lesbian Chamber of Commerce, I realized how important it is for me to stay visible and to get comfortable with making my voice heard. Each time I share my story, I'm hoping that it gives the little black trans boy at the back of the room an opportunity to say, "Hey, there is somebody that looks like me!" I want them to feel like they don't have to hide. If they decide to be stealth, that's fine, but making sure they know that they're not alone is important. It's my mission to be a resource for my community and offer them the help I wish I would've had early on. It is scary to be vulnerable, accessible, cataloged, and possibly rejected. But that's what makes me resilient.

My work with the NGLCC has now expanded into the Transgender and Gender Non-Conforming Task Force Mentorship Committee, where we mentor other trans and gender nonconforming business owners. What makes this work so powerful, is that these business owners are offered resources to help them thrive.

LOVE LOST AND REGAINED

Experiencing a loss of relationships after making the decision to transition is normal. I lost a multitude of friends and family members. Growing up, I admired my older brother and we were so close. I never would have imagined that our relationship would be impacted by my transition. I became the black sheep of the family, ostracized from the rest.

One of the people I wanted to contact was my grandmother. It had been about 15 years since I had seen her and I wanted her to see who I had become. I never got that opportunity, because my aunt prohibited me from seeing her before she died. I attended her funeral, but it was brutal. It was devastating and cruel, the way my family treated me like a stranger at my own grandmother's funeral. Like I was a bystander that happened to find their way into the wrong family cookout. I got tired of explaining who I was to family members, only to be met with confusion and disdain—it added to the pain that I was already experiencing. It makes me think back to my friend Shane and how he told me his family accepted him with ease.

The theme of acceptance amongst POC in the LGBT community is an ongoing and ever-evolving conversation. As a black parent I have to ask...In what ways do our kids need us? And have we failed to rise to the occasion of their need?

As people of color we have to do better with how we love each other. Love has to be irrevocable and not based on conditions where they get the option of deciding whether your infraction makes you unlovable.

Even given all of the highs and lows in the relationship with my mother, we have mended what was once broken. Through all of the arguments, I realized we were fighting for understanding and reconciliation. We talk every day and there isn't a day that goes by that she doesn't call me her best friend. Although she still calls me by my birth name in private, she never gets it wrong in public. The early years of my transition were spent living in shame about being born a woman, but now I am so grateful I had the opportunity to live two full lives in one lifetime. I have embraced being queer and I hope that more people learn how to love all of their parts because those are the things that make us unique.

From conversations I've had with my mother over the years, I've learned that trans people and their families have to grant each other some grace and patience. For example, while I had known since elementary school that I was transgender, my mom only learned of it recently. For her, it must've seemed like a drastic change, when for me, I had many more years to understand it. I had to learn to give her grace. As trans people, we have to be a little more gracious with our parents in allowing them to transition with us. I know that not every parent will come around. Some need more time than others. Time, communication, and a commitment to trying oftentimes repairs relationships.

Conversations with my mother look different today. There isn't anything we don't talk about because there isn't anything that can destroy us. That's what we all need—an open door to ask and learn.

WHERE I STAND NOW

Today, more than ever, I feel like the man that I always wanted to be, that I always knew I was. I'm happy with my physical body, my mental body, my spiritual body. They're all working as one cohesive unit. My story is a story of resilience. I often share my story, not to have anyone focus on *what* I went through but rather *how* I went through it.

The joy that I have isn't tied to relationships or others' acceptance of me. It's just tied to my relationship with myself and the realization that I *am* enough and I always will be. We all have our days where we experience discomfort, but those days do pass and every morning is pregnant with new opportunities.

Every day, there's a shift—every day offers a new lesson and I show up eager to live at the level of the soul. I've come through the fire and I don't even smell like smoke!

BECOMING UNFUCKWITHABLE

My advice for other trans men is to find your voice and find your community. Take a whole seat at the table. Don't just stand next to the table, take a seat. Walk your truth, whatever that is for you—create yourself. You will go through several transitions within your transition. Your mindset will transition along with your physical body. For example, at one point I thought, *I'll never want to have hair on my face*, and now I have a Moses beard. I also never imagined I would allow my hair to grow down my back.

For any trans men of color who may read this: Make sure that you're asking yourself some deep questions about who you want to be. Find a mentor who can help you along your path. Lastly, know that you don't have to follow the archetypes that other men have laid out, because there is no one way to be a man. This is your experience, your life, and you are the only one who gets to decide how you're going to live it.

Gavriel Legynd

KAI BERZINSKAS

Kai Berzinskas (he/him) is a developmental special-ist pursuing a Ph.D. in educational psychology with a concentration in mental health counseling. Kai's journey has given him the groundwork to fill a void in the lack of therapists catering to the LGBTI com-munity, especially the trans community. His goals are to work specifically with the LGBTI community as a mental health counselor, helping others overcome the struggles of living an authentic life.

GRAPPLING AND COMING TO TERMS

At a very young age, I didn't want to be a girl. By the age of three or four years old, I didn't like 'girly' things, nor did I want to play with them. Instead, I'd follow the boys around, doing the things that they were doing and playing with their toys. Sometimes I'd try to take my shirt off like them, which didn't always go over too well with my parents. Growing up in the '70s, there weren't any people that I could relate to or words that could describe how I felt, other than being a 'tomboy.' The only famous trans person was Renée Richards, the former tennis star, whose publicized transition wasn't widely talked about. Even when a trans person was brought up, it was usually reducing that person to a quick punch line or talking about trans sex workers.

So when I told my parents that I wanted to be a boy, they just ignored it. In their minds, they probably thought, *Oh that'll never happen.* To them, it was probably no different than if I'd said I'd wanted to be a mermaid. I was just a kid pretending. Still, the tomboyish behavior never stopped. In school, I continued to imitate the boys, how they looked and acted. By fifth grade, as a result of my dyslexia, I began working with a psychologist, who took it upon himself to also "correct" my boyish behavior. He made me wear dresses three out of five days of the week; if I didn't comply, then I couldn't play soccer at my school. At the time, soccer was my go-to way I could express myself, even though I could only play on the girls' team. Now, thanks to the psychologist, it was being taken away from me.

His influence also spurred my parents to take things away from me if I didn't comply with how he thought I should dress and act. So I was forced to be very feminine, carrying purses and "acting like a girl should." I couldn't swear because girls didn't swear. I couldn't even say certain words without backlash. During the 1970s, this was a form of conversion therapy and it continued on for nearly two years, making them some of the hardest experiences I went through as a child. Being forced into a box that I knew I didn't fit in, but given no choice otherwise.

It cut deep and left a permanent mark on me.

THE AFTERMATH: LOVE, ALCOHOL, AND COMING OUT

In the aftermath of my childhood, I felt that I could only follow the path that was laid out by society for people assigned female at birth: you go through school; get married; have a kid or two; and become a housewife, with your only focus being the family. Remember, this was the 1970s, and at the time, there weren't any resources like the internet or social media that people could turn to and find others like them who might be going through similar experiences. To even mention being trans to another person was enough to get you killed. It was like being on an island, isolated. So I did what others did and followed that typical path—I got married, became a housewife, and had a son.

Complying with this path didn't mean I was happy. I turned to alcohol to cope, not only with my marriage, but with what we now know was an identity struggle. Though my husband and I tried to make things work over the years, I realized that I liked women. Since I was still identifying as a woman, at this point I came out as gay, which was (perhaps) an easier path for the times. Shortly after, I divorced, and found a new place to live and a new partner in the lesbian community.

After the divorce, I met and married a woman. There were periods of time where I would be sober, but I'd often relapse with emotional and financial struggles, enough that I accepted that I was an alcoholic and needed help. I began rehab and attended Alcoholics Anonymous (AA) meetings. The meetings gave me a support group that helped me along in my journey. This was also the first time I met someone transgender. Hearing their stories and where they came from, I related to a lot of it. What they felt like when they were growing up and the feelings they repressed for years, because they didn't have the language to describe what they were feeling or how they'd faced the fear of the social repercussions of being trans.

Relating so much to their story, I asked myself—*Am I trans or is this something else?* I grappled with it for a long time, before I met a close friend, a trans man, whom I really admired. The more time I spent with him, the more I wanted to be like him; I became envious of him. Through the meetings, we ended up talking more and more, getting closer. One day, we sat down for coffee, and I opened up about my feelings that I might be transgender.

He said, "I have a feeling that within a year, you are going to be on hormones and going through your transition."

Him saying that really sunk in and made me think about everything in my life. It was validating and surprising to hear him say that and made me realize that I related to all the trans stories I was hearing because I was also trans. Suddenly, I began to see that everything up to this point in my life were signs that I was trans, and as I connected the dots, I knew what I wanted to do going forward.

COMING CLEAN

My biggest concern with transitioning was how it would affect my family and the people around me. While times had changed a little, being transgender was still not accepted or readily talked about. I had my kid to worry about, as well as my job and coworkers, and my wife. What would be their reactions? Would they treat me the same way or differently—or cut me out of their lives completely? How would they fair out in the world? My son was then 11 years old, and like all parents, I was really concerned about how he would feel and take it. We had a strong relationship, but I was scared that he would reject me and not be accepting.

When I opened up to him, I explained who I was and who I wanted to be, and I tried to simplify it by saying that I wanted to be a boy.

He reacted by screaming, "My mom wants to be a boy!"

Over time, though, with lots of talks, he grew to accept who I was. But in the moment, it was a lot for a kid to take in. Looking back, I probably could've done it a lot smoother, or consulted a therapist on the best way to approach it. Maybe if books were more readily available back then, for him or me, it would've been different.

Coming out to my wife was challenging, but since we had friends who were transitioning, she understood what it meant to transition and accepted me for me. I ended up also telling my ex-husband, since we were both still connected and parenting a child together. He seemed to understand, but was mostly concerned with how it would affect my son.

In those first few months of telling people, I explained that I wasn't ready for the drastic changes that went with starting HRT. I wanted the people around me to slowly adjust to the changes that would come. I'd suggested that I'd take only a small amount of testosterone cream, and have the changes appear slowly, but my son and my ex-husband both objected. They wanted me to wait until my son had graduated high school. I understood the reasoning behind their concerns. Changes were going to happen and that could spill over onto my son's life. The last thing I'd wanted was for him to be bullied or treated differently because of me.

My father had a similar reaction as my son when I told him. Being of an even older generation, he didn't understand where this "idea" came from. For him, it was like being trans came out of nowhere, even though I'd grown up in his house-hold, having these feelings and behaviors the entire time; I just didn't have the words for it at the time to explain it to others. Trying to explain what everything meant, what I was going through, and how I felt about everything really took a while. Both he and my mother thought that they did something wrong and didn't understand what I was going through. My mom blamed herself, thinking of every little thing that could've led to this, like somehow one "mistake" when I was five led me to transition decades later. They were both worried and confused about why I would go through this.

During those first months of coming out, I thought to myself that my life was going to be manageable if I just transitioned socially and not medically, that I could wait until my son graduated. But the dysphoria was pilling up and weighing on me. It came to a point where I realized that I would relapse again, and truthfully, my mental health was already not well. I talked with my son and my wife, and told them that I needed to do this in stages and that I wanted to do it together. I explained to them that I needed to live an authentic life. That it meant I was going to have a beard and not shave it off to hide my being trans. Life was too short and I wanted to be happy.

In the end, I pursued it; I knew that transitioning was the only way to move forward. And I set up an appointment with an endocrinologist. My AA friend was right: within the year, I'd started taking testosterone and began transitioning.

BEING FORCED INTO A BOX THAT I KNEW I DIDN'T FIT IN, BUT GIVEN NO CHOICE OTHERWISE CUT DEEP AND LEFT A PERMANENT MARK ON ME.

TAKING THINGS IN STAGES

My son, wife, and I started to go to therapy in the earlier parts of my transition. It gave them time to adjust to the changes that were coming our way and how to handle different situations that might arise, like if my son or wife had friends over or if we went out in public. It helped them adjust to the person I was becoming. However, I did become more secluded and tried to make sure that my transition wouldn't have any negative impact on my son's life, even if that meant being seen publicly for who I was by other people had to take a backseat.

In a way, my son transitioned with me. We were both becoming the men we were meant to be. For me, it was medically and for him it was growing up and getting older. After about two years going to family therapy, the therapist said that there wasn't a need for my son to be there anymore, that he had come to terms with me and my transition. Knowing that, it felt like one thing was going right for me during my transition.

Despite my son's acceptance, those first two years were some of the hardest that I had to endure. It was a difficult process, coming out to people and getting people to recognize me now as Kai. Acceptance was the biggest struggle, since I was in the awkward stage of just starting hormones, only two years on testosterone. Especially since I was taking a smaller dose of testosterone, the changes—from body-fat redistribution, voice deepening, to starting to grow facial hair—all happened slower.

After about two years of taking minimal amounts of HRT, I felt as if my life was on standstill. Not being out at my job, I would constantly be referred to as 'she' or 'ma'am,' and it piled on like getting punched in the gut. I had to act like nothing was wrong because if I made a big deal out of it, that would draw more attention and more people would misgender me. This was on top of trying to please everyone, to take things slowly enough that my family and I were comfortable but it was taking a toll on me.

My boobs were causing a huge amount of gender dysphoria and I knew that I needed to have top surgery. That was a definitive turning point for my family and in my life. Once I had surgery, I couldn't go back. I wasn't out to my job, but there had been multiple people who had gotten double mastectomies and were still seen as feminine. I figured I wouldn't be seen as masculine immediately and just like with the other areas of my life, I would take it slow in the workplace. Eventually, I scheduled an appointment for the surgery, then told both my family and job.

Once the surgery was over, I felt so much happier; I had finally taken this huge step forward in my transition. But that happiness was cut short by my wife.

Shortly after the recovery period, we discussed our relationship. She explained that we'd met when I was very feminine; now I was stepping very far away from that. The dynamic between us was already shifting, and in her eyes, I wasn't the same person that she'd met and married. In the end, the top surgery was too much for her and she left. Although she still cared for me, it felt like the progress I'd made was blown away by losing one of the people closest to me. I fell back into a dark place, and began to relapse, and later attend AA meetings and rehab. It was extremely difficult, but I thankfully had my son and my recovery friends there to support me.

My son was my biggest supporter throughout all of this. We've been there for each other through all the struggles. He's been extremely supportive of me going to meetings and in my recovery in general. During those dark periods, he helped me get back on track and encouraged me to continue my sobriety. I was also lucky that a lot of the friends that I'd met through recovery were also trans or gay or lesbian, giving me a place to share stories, experiences, and advice.

As time went on, sharing our lived experiences taught me to have more appreciation and love for myself after what I'd been through, and continue to go through. Those heart-to-heart moments with other trans people pushed me to see that I needed to live my life for me. If people had a problem with the way I dressed or who I was, then that was their problem to deal with and not something I needed to invest time or energy into. People either accept it or don't—regardless, I'm going to continue living my life.

LIVING LIFE FOR ME

Around the time my son was in his sophomore year of high school, he sat me down for a chat.

He said, "You know, Mom, I forgot how this all came about, but you know I'm really cool with you transitioning. I have a lot of friends who are gay and some trans friends and I'm really cool with it."

Hearing that from him, the validation that no matter what, he was going to be by my side really touched my heart. It made me think that everything was really going to be okay after all.

Out in public, he'll use he/him, Kai, or parent, when referring to me, but in private, when it's just the two of us, he occasionally calls me 'mom.' We have a great relationship and for him, he will always see me as his mom, and that's fine with me. We joke and play it off sometimes. It's something that doesn't bother me and something that works out for the both of us. This isn't to say that every trans parent should have this specific dynamic with their child, but that this is our dynamic and it works for us. He's my biggest supporter in everything that I do, through every milestone; even in the darker periods, he's been there every step of the way.

As I was moving forward in my transition with the full support of my son, I knew that I needed to finally address the elephant in the room with my parents. I kept trying to get them to understand more about me and my transition through the years, but nothing seemed to stick.

It wasn't until I shared Chaz Bono's book with them that they started to open up. They got to really understand what it's like to be a transgender person and to go through transition. Chaz is the trans son of the famous performer Cher, a star in my parents' generation. That was the gateway that opened up dialogue with my parents.

From Chaz's biography, they began to understand what it was like for me to be a transgender person and go through transition. They would ask me tons of questions, like if I'd experienced or dealt with the things that Chaz had. It gave them the foundation to understand me through the lens of someone like me.

Today, they are very supportive. My mother even attends PFLAG meetings, the organization comprised of Parents and Friends of Lesbians and Gays; she's also part of a transgender support group. I'm lucky that they came around and now accept and support me for who I am.

Chaz's book also opened up conversations about what happened when I was younger and the conversion therapy they put me through. They were able to empathize with me and recognize how much it hurt and how deep of a scar it left on my heart.

At the time, they thought what they were doing was right. When I was growing up in the '70s, there wasn't widely used language to describe transgender people, and there weren't as many public stories or resources as there are today. Nevertheless, they understood how much harm that did and apologized for putting me through that. I know that apologies can only cover up so much, but it felt like closure to know that they finally recognized what they did and put me through.

We continued to have more conversations and more questions kept coming up as I continued to provide them with resources to help them understand my experiences and what I'm going through on a daily basis. One of the more pivotal books that I gave them was *Trans Bodies, Trans Selves*, which really outlines what a trans person goes through socially, medically, physically, and mentally. It provided a ton of different stories and perspectives that helped them understand who I am and that this is who I've always been.

My parents have come a long way. They still sometimes mess up my pronouns and call me 'she' or say "sh—he" really quickly and I laugh about it and let it roll off my back. They're in their seventies now. They'd been calling me 'she' and 'her' for their entire lives, and then I came in and threw a wrench in that. I'm grateful though, that they support me and accept me for who I am, even if they mess up now and then. Knowing I have their support, it feels like a weight was lifted off of me. Now I can live my life as me around my parents and have my parents with me as I continue to grow into the person I've always been.

BEING TRANS IN THE WORKPLACE

The next step I knew that I needed to take to live authentically was for me to completely come out to my workplace. In 2014, I was going to get my name changed after already having gotten top surgery in 2013. Top surgery was the most visible change that I made so far; that brought a lot of looks and a lot of questions about what happened and if I was okay. I let people know that I was okay and that I had done it for personal reasons, which seemed to satisfy a majority of the people I was working with. When I got my name changed, everyone seemed fine with it; there wasn't a barrage of questions or people interrogating me about why I went through with it.

Within a year of changing my name and officially presenting myself to the world as Kai, I switched from the gel-form of HRT to shots, changed my gender marker, and came out fully at my job. I was tired of hiding who I was, and eventually I had to decide whether I was all in or all out. I went all in, feeling like, *This is who I am, I'm not hiding anymore.* I had the support from my family that I'd needed and if my coworkers didn't like it, then it was their problem to deal with.

Actually coming out to my job and letting them know I was transitioning was a bit bumpy. A lot of people there accepted and respected me with the exception of a few people.

One person tried to claim that I wasn't trans enough saying like, "Really? You're transitioning? You don't even have facial hair."

This was just around the time of me starting injections. I felt like I had to explain myself but I took a step back. *We're at work! Who are you to question me about my transition?* I realized it wasn't worth the time and energy to explain myself to someone who doesn't really care. By the time I was completely out in my workplace, I felt exhausted.

Ironically, I changed my gender marker around the time my job was transferring me to a new department. The new department basically knew nothing about me and it was almost as if I was starting on a clean slate in a way. The HR Department had already made the introductions for me and gave a little bit of a background on me, including the fact that I'm trans. Since then it's been great. Most of my co-workers use he/him, nobody questions me when I use the men's bathroom.

There are those one or two co-workers that use she and I think that's because of my voice; maybe they are trying to disrespect me, but I don't let it get to me. Outside of work, I get called 'he' and 'sir' all the time, so the people who are being disrespectful look like they're the weird ones. I knew that I was on the right path. Being on shots instead of the low-dose gel, I knew that I would start to grow a beard and that my voice would deepen. But above all, I knew I didn't need anyone else's approval.

It wasn't until these past few years that I finally said, "You know what? I don't care what people think, I'm doing this for me." I'm going to live an authentic life. I'm going to do this because this is what I want and I don't care what society thinks. Life is too short and I've waited too long to be happy.

LOOKING BACK AND MOVING FORWARD

Looking back at everything as I'm writing this, I can truly say that I'm happy now. I'm now about a year sober, and I feel confident in my body. I can actually look in the mirror, smile, and be happy at what I see. I mean, it'd be nice if I could lose a little weight and add some muscle, but that's beside the point. I have an extremely supportive son, who accepts me and supports me throughout all aspects of my life, and I him. My son is now 18 and he is still my biggest supporter. He's said that he accepts the fact that he has a transgender parent. My coworkers are accepting. I have a supportive dad and an enthusiastic mom. I'm able to support and be there for other people who are struggling with alcoholism and through their transitions.

A friend of mine and I are actually trying to educate more when we go to AA meetings. Unfortunately, being openly trans or LGBTQ+ is still "new" in the recovery community, so there have been times where people have said homophobic and transphobic things while we've been trying to educate and share our stories. In a way, we're letting other people there know that, "Hey, LGBTQ+ people may be here," and their stories and identities are just as valid as everyone else in the room.

Thinking about the experiences that I've had and talking with many other trans people, I know I'm one of the lucky ones. The people in my life are wonderful and accept me for who I am, but I know this isn't the case for everyone. I read a blog for trans men who are my age, and I hear a lot of unfortunate stories where people have lost their families and struggle with addiction and alcoholism. Homelessness, poverty, suicide; all of this is very real in the trans community and happens far too often.

I'M GOING TO **LIVE AN AUTHENTIC LIFE.** I'M GOING TO DO THIS BECAUSE THIS IS WHAT I WANT AND I DON'T CARE WHAT SOCIETY THINKS. **LIFE IS TOO SHORT AND I'VE WAITED TOO LONG TO BE HAPPY.**

This is part of the reason why I want to do what I can for the trans and LGBTQ+ community. That's why, as of writing this, I'm going back to school for my doctorate in educational psychology to become a licensed mental health counselor. I was fortunate enough to have a supportive therapist who worked with me and my family through transition, but I've also been put through conversion therapy with another. It's a mixed bag; there are some really transphobic and homophobic therapists out there but there are some that are outstanding allies or have gone through similar experiences themselves.

My hope is that I can help LGBTQ+ people who need a therapist they can trust and relate to about what they are going through, and that I can help them be the person they are. I carry the same hope in sharing my story in this book: That it helps provide hope for anyone who has struggled or is struggling, to know that there is a light at the end of the tunnel and getting there is absolutely worth it.

For any trans person reading this, my advice to you is to live your life with no regrets. Don't get caught up in society's expectations of who you should be or what you should do. Do the things you want to do, not for other people, but for yourself. Pursue the dreams that you have and live your life the way you see fit. We have a place in society, just like anybody else. So just hold on and go at your own pace.

Transition is by no means all rainbows and smiles, but take solace in where you are. This should be a fun time, where you come into your authentic self and start to learn who you are. It's filled with discovery, finding community, and being happy with yourself. It's not something that has a set start and end date, but something that continues on as we get to know ourselves. Live as authentically as possible and, above all, live your truth.

These are all things that I wish I could've told my younger self, on top of telling myself to hang in there and that everything would work out. It's easy to look back and say that of course everything was going to be fine, but hearing that is what I feel like I needed the most. I wish that I could've transitioned earlier, but I was born in the '70s, without the luxury of the internet. And now, here I am, surrounded by people who love and accept me.

I may not be able to tell that to my past self, but I can tell anyone who is reading this. Whatever you're going through, no matter how tough it is, you can get through this. Everything will work out in the end and you will be at the place that you want to be. My hope for anyone reading this is that it has helped open your mind and given you hope that, no matter the obstacles, you can make it in this world as your authentic self.

Kai Berzinskas

BRAXTON T. FLEMING

Braxton T. Fleming (he/him) is a Licensed Practicing Nurse (LPN). He is also the CEO and Founder of Stealth Bros. &Co., an online Luxury Medical supply company that provides personal storage bags for hormone replacement therapy (HRT) supplies, for easy-to-travel and at home use. Started from his room in 2018, Stealth Bros. &Co. continues to grow and serve the transgender community and allies, and even offers a surgery fund for those in the LGBTQ+ community in need. By sharing his experiences, Braxton hopes to inspire other trans people on their journeys and to fill a gap in representation of trans people of color.

STRUGGLING TO FIND MYSELF

Growing up, I felt closest with my dad. He's always supported me in my endeavors and throughout my life. I grew up with my dad, sister, and grandmother. But a lot of the time, when my parents were working, my godparents would watch over me, my sister, godsister, and five godbrothers. Spending time with all of them, I always felt more connected to my godbrothers than my sisters. I would try to do everything that my godbrothers were doing, from the games they were playing to the way they acted.

I remember being in my bed at night, wishing that I was a boy like them so that I could do everything that they were doing. My godparents took notice and would try and nudge me to spend more time with my sisters and do the things that they were doing instead. If I gravitated back to my godbrothers, they would redirect me to do 'girly' things with my sisters. I quickly learned that there was something different about me that separated me from my godbrothers.

Thankfully, my dad was super chill and never tried to redirect or stop me from doing 'boy' things. In fact, he was always teaching me to do the jobs that he was doing. He never corrected me when I did 'boyish' things, like wearing basketball shorts, cutting the grass, or changing the car's oil. Sure, I couldn't run around with my shirt off or go pee in the woods, like my godbrothers, but with my dad, I got to express that part of me—the part that was different.

When I got to college, I was faced with new obstacles to figuring out my place in the world. The college was Kean University in Union, NJ. I was enrolled in classes to become a nurse, a field I thought fit me. In my classes, I was surrounded by other students, who were a welcoming group of people but assumed that I was a lesbian. I had a very androgynous look, which is what led them to assume but it's also what led me to start questioning myself. For me, I felt like, *No, of course I'm not a lesbian*, but then I started thinking about it and questioning—*Am I a lesbian?* Even though the word 'lesbian' didn't resonate with me, I began a relationship with a woman, which I tried to do without labeling myself—but it happened anyway. That label felt counter to who I felt I was and as a result, I was angry at people a lot of the time for putting it on me. On the inside, I was just me.

Throughout my life, I felt as if no one respected me because I wasn't getting seen the same way as I felt. I was a 98-pound, mad little thing. People would try and help me with the smallest things, like carrying a heavy box or carrying in the groceries, and I'd be like, "No! I don't need your help!" People saw my size and treated me like I was a child, as if they thought I couldn't do things or handle things by myself and felt a need to help. Looking back, I can't blame them; that was how they were taught to see me. But it was killing me on the inside—I was frustrated that they couldn't see me for who I was. In the end, it caused me to fall into a dark hole. I didn't know who I was or what I was doing.

When I try to explain to people what it was like, I tell them I felt like a fetus. I was asking myself, *Why do I still look like I'm a child at 27 years old?* It was like I wasn't growing—physically or personally. I thought maybe I'd find the answer by focusing on my nursing career or that I needed a hobby. Soon after I graduated, I started to do research into different jobs and even buying stocks, thinking that these might be an answer to what I felt was missing and could complete me. But it didn't help and only deepened the dark hole. Thankfully, by some chance coincidence, I came upon a YouTube video about trans people while I was researching careers. That's when everything started to click for me.

COMING INTO MY OWN

The YouTube video featured a trans man talking about how he knew he was transgender. I related to all the things that he was saying; things about his childhood and growing up, and how he felt different as a child, and didn't realize what it all meant until later in life. His childhood was very similar to mine, and the more I watched, the more I ended up crying. Everything finally clicked for me and I realized at that moment that this was my life. I was transgender.

After that first video, I started to watch tons of videos by other trans men who were describing their own experiences. They would talk about what it was like for them growing up, how they knew who they were, what it was like coming out, going through medical transition, and where they are now. I watched other trans men's transitions, as they recorded their progress once they'd started hormone replacement therapy (HRT). Typically, as I learned, trans men received their testosterone through injection with a needle. I would check back for their weekly or monthly updates about the changes they were going through, and I would see things that excited me, like the deepening of their voices, the growth of facial hair, and overall, just looking more like men. It was from those videos that I started to explore and learn more about what it means to be transgender and be part of the transgender community as a whole.

The more I learned and took everything in, the more I knew that I needed to start HRT. It was the change I was looking for—and just the possibility of becoming the person I had always wanted to be made everything in my life up to this point make sense. All the childhood struggles with why I felt that I was never growing, why I felt so angry all the time, or why it was so natural I was trying to imitate my godbrothers and my dad, it all now made sense to me. What I was searching for was brotherhood and belonging in a community of people. Just like I never fit in as a lesbian, I had this deep knowing that inside there was always something different about me. For the first time, I found a place where I didn't feel different. Pieces were falling into place and I knew the community that I had been searching for was the trans community.

FOR THE FIRST TIME, I FOUND A PLACE WHERE I DIDN'T FEEL DIFFERENT. PIECES WERE FALLING INTO PLACE AND I KNEW THE COMMUNITY THAT I HAD BEEN SEARCHING FOR WAS THE TRANS COMMUNITY.

Another thought came to me that I wasn't expecting. Reviewing my life, I saw how important it was being around my dad. Up until this point, it never occurred to me that I wanted to be a father of my own children, to take the lessons that he'd passed onto me and give them to kids of my own. Thinking more about it, I started craving the feeling of being a Dad. In a way, I'd known it deep down, but didn't have the words to express it in a way that made sense to me. Now I did.

After learning more about what it means to be trans and what trans people go through (e.g., HRT, coming out, name change, surgeries, socially transitioning, and becoming ourselves), I made an appointment with a therapist, who needed to sign off saying I had gender dysphoria in order to recommend me for HRT. After a couple of sessions, and working through the new things I was learning about myself, I started to medically transition.

During that time, my body wasn't the only thing HRT was affecting. The emotional swings from HRT were also taking effect. My emotions would bounce around constantly, going from feeling down about myself to being okay for a few hours. After a while, my emotions weren't as erratic, but I still felt depressed a lot of the time. On the one hand, I was still coming into my own, but since the big physical changes from HRT hadn't taken effect yet, I was still being misgendered constantly, as in being called 'her' or 'ma'am.' I don't hold it against people, but it still hurt.

Those first few months were some of the hardest. I would still watch other trans men's transition videos, studying them, thinking that at x-time I'd finally have this major change and I wouldn't be misgendered as much, or that I'd finally feel good about myself once I hit x-month. Instead, I was met with constant disappointment and depression when things didn't line up exactly like I'd thought. I wanted to be at the end goal so badly. I kept envisioning myself there, only to look in a mirror and see how far I still had to go.

The next step for me was to socially transition and come out to the people close to me. When I opened up to my close friends, they took me in and supported me. Some needed an explanation about what it meant to be trans or needed time to adjust to my "new" self. Others adjusted easily, since they knew other people who were trans or learned the stories of prominent trans people like Laverne Cox. Coming out to my dad was harder.

I was terrified to tell the man who taught me so much and helped me come into my own. I was scared what his response would be to me coming out as trans. When I finally did get up the courage to tell him, he was upset, but not for the reason that I thought. He was upset because he wasn't able to help me transition earlier as a child, so I could already be who I am today. He saw who I was when I was younger but, just like me, he didn't have all the answers—or rather, he didn't have the words to describe who I was. Hearing that from him, it was an emotional moment for both of us, and I was so happy to have him in my corner.

ENDINGS TO MAKE WAY FOR BEGINNINGS

At the time of my transition, I was in an eight-year relationship with my girlfriend and, as supportive as she was during that time, it ultimately wasn't the healthiest. We had become very codependent on one another. To her, I was stagnant and not doing anything with my life. She couldn't understand the struggle I was going through as being part of this journey. When I finally did tell her I was trans, she was supportive at first, never misgendering me or calling me by my old name, like some people did.

But during my first year on hormones, the tension between us increased, and she began to grieve as if she'd lost me. It took her time to adjust to this new person that I was becoming. Even though I was still the same person, it was the outward appearance and the visible changes happening day-to-day that made her think that I was becoming someone entirely different.

A few months before my one-year anniversary of being on HRT, we broke up. It was my darkest moment because all the experiences and memories that we'd had together ended abruptly. Now I was the one grieving the loss of her. I cried for months after we broke up. I loved her with every fiber of my being. I ended up moving back in with my dad after we broke up and I began to dig deep to figure out who I was and what I was going to do with my life from that point onward.

THE START OF A BUSINESS

When I was younger, my dad and I would talk about moving to Florida because we both hated the cold. He was an entrepreneur, and we often talked about ways we could make the money to get down there. He always said to become rich, you needed to serve a need. His idea was to invent something.

In his words, "You don't make a product that people want; you make something that people need." That stuck with me throughout my entire life.

After moving back home, I began to focus on building myself up. I finally felt that I knew who I was as a person and that I just needed to keep moving forward. I took a job as an LPN, doing Pediatric Home Care Nursing. I had been sitting on an idea for a business for months but didn't have the time to bring it to life until I started working as a Home Care Nurse. Watching videos of other trans men, I took note of how they would leave their needles lying around instead of in a safe location. That was when an idea for a new business hit me: a readily accessible bag to store HRT needles. I knew this was something that I wanted to do and I finally was able to sit down and work out the details.

Even for people who take medication regularly, like insulin, there isn't an over-the-counter bag that you can buy to safely and discreetly store the medicine and supplies. I started researching how much each bag would cost and who could manufacture a large quantity of bags. Once I found a manufacturer, I started to think about how I would distribute the bags, what I'd do for a website, and how to advertise that they even existed. I settled on promoting on social media to start and came up with the name of the business, Stealth Bros. & Co. I wanted a name that reflected 'brotherhood,' because of how important it was to me.

I remember the day I told my dad about the company. I was outside cutting the grass. He was on the second floor looking out the window, as I yelled to him the logistics: how much it costs vs. how much I was going to sell each bag for, and how I was going to buy 300 bags to start with.

His immediate response was, "Are you sure 300 bags is going to be enough?"

How amazing is that! I told him that I should be able to sell the full amount within the year and within two months, I sold all 300 of those bags.

Since those first few months, Stealth Bros. has continued to grow, and I'm continually stunned at the number of people that it has helped. Within two years, we've sold nearly 4,000 products. I've read comments that people leave on our social media saying, "Thank you," or sharing how they feel so much more comfortable taking their medicine with them. Hearing stories like how someone felt much more comfortable going through TSA with a Stealth Bros. bag, or how it even reminded some people that they need to take their HRT, makes me feel like it was all worth it—the struggle, the fight, the climb I took to become me. The long nights, the razor sharp determination, and consistent effort I put into building what SBC is today, it all paid off.

Today, every time I hear another story from someone we've helped, it pushes me to do more and keep advancing. All the people that I've met and the connections I've made around the country through my business and brand have been incredible. I've done modeling through my business, and even attended New York Fashion Week. I've created an Instagram account @sire.brax where I offer motivational snippets on IG stories called *The Brax Car Talk*, to share moments from my day with others. Stealth Bros. has also given me a platform to share my story so others can be inspired, educated, and motivated.

My goal is to always help other people (both trans and cis) in some way. It's still hard, since I work a full-time job and manage every aspect of Stealth Bros. by myself. But knowing that it continues to impact people is what keeps me going. Since starting Stealth Bros., we've added a transition surgery fund. Part of the proceeds are collected into a fund that'll be awarded to someone who needs help paying for gender affirming transition-related surgeries and supplies. Looking back at everything in my life, it's crazy how far I've come, and yet, I continue to challenge myself to keep growing.

ALWAYS GROWING AND FILLING A GAP

On my one-year anniversary of being on HRT, with Stealth Bros. taking off, I felt like everything was working out. I was already one year on T, had a full beard, and I was really coming into myself. People were finally seeing me as I saw myself. Random people were no longer misgendering me and when they did, *they* would look like the weird one, because everyone read me as a man.

I also celebrated the day by rewatching a video I'd made when I was just one month in, where I asked my future self questions like how is life, was transition what I expected, and what changes had I experienced?

If I could go back and talk to my past self, I would've said, "Just chill out; everything's going to be okay."

I wanted to tell myself to just enjoy the process and not to stop, because at one-year, I was at the point in my journey where I'd wanted to be for so long.

To me, the experiences that I have had, good and bad, were part of the learning experience and me growing as a person. Dealing with the day-to-day struggles of coming out to my friends and explaining my transition to others—those were part of my journey. Eventually, I reached a point where I knew who I was and it was on the other person to respect that. I didn't need to spend time and energy trying to convince anyone about who I was, or keep them comfortable enough to accept me. You don't have to understand everything about my life to accept who I am.

As of writing this, I'm in my third year of being on HRT, and looking back at everything that happened, I know that the person that I was before is still with me. I know for some trans people, they want to forget that part of their life because that wasn't who they were, but for me, I loved that person. That person is still within me. Like, I don't mind talking about my old name or saying who I was as a person. I feel that having that female experience for 27 years of my life was necessary; now I have both perspectives. Plus, it helps me to know what a woman really likes and needs and how to handle certain things that can come up. So I don't like to degrade that part of me or say, "No, that person's dead," because that person is always with me.

Looking back, I've had a really blessed experience. Maybe my story isn't the case for so many trans men and trans people of color. I have had multiple people ask me if I had to deal with racism as a black man, especially as a black trans man, or if I've had any encounters with people who were spewing racist bigotry. Luckily, I haven't; the people that I've told my story to and the people that I've interacted with have been respectful. There's the occasional offhand comment, but most people quickly apologize and listen when I confront them.

While I've been fortunate enough to not face racism, I have noticed a huge lack of diversity within the trans men community. During my transition, I found it hard to find someone who looked like me, someone who had a similar skin tone as mine. When I did, I felt that I truly related to them. Out of hundreds of transition videos I watched, only a handful were of trans men of color. This might be because of an unspoken non-acceptance of queerness in general in the POC community. I knew that needed to change, that I needed to share my story and represent for others like me. Though it's changed in the past few years, more can be done to increase visibility for trans people of color. Either way, I'm proud to be a part of it.

LOOKING AHEAD

For any trans person that's reading this, my biggest advice to you is to try not to compare your transition to others, even though that's the hardest thing to do. I know I used to do it. I would obsess over other guys' transitions and, when things weren't happening for me, I was disappointed and upset that my transition wasn't going how I thought it was "supposed to."

I have gotten a lot of people reaching out to me asking, "Oh, how do I get there? How do I get there in my transition?"

I tried to tell them to accept who you are and where you are in your life. It's your own personal journey—just accept it for where it's at in that moment of time.

Try not to rush the transition process or think that major change will happen in x-amount of time. It's just not worth it, because you'll just end up being disappointed if you don't meet that goal at a certain time like someone else did. Everyone's body is different.

That's something that I tell trans people who are just starting out: "Just chill out." Everything will happen for you when it's meant for you. It's not easy, nothing that's worth having is easy. The hardest part is waiting. Waiting for changes to come in, for people to come around, waiting to get to where you know you need to be.

For other trans men of color who can relate to my story, I hope you know you aren't alone. There are people like you, who share a similar background, and have also struggled to find themselves. I want you to know that it's okay.

If there's one takeaway from my story, it's that you can do anything you put your mind to. As long as you can see what you want to do or who you want to be, and you're actively working towards it, I feel like you can do it. You can achieve what you set your mind to. You can build a business, right inside your bedroom, and make a change in others' lives and help them through their journeys. You can go from 98-pounds to 135 and look good doing it. Whatever you're passionate about or whoever you want to be, you can do it; you can be the change that you need in your life to get you to where you need to be.

There will be times where you feel like you don't want to be here anymore, but those are the times that you have to go through to be strong and get to where you want to be. No matter where you are in your life, if you keep going and keep pushing, you will get to that point in your life that you're envisioning for yourself.

If I can do it, so can you.

Braxton T. Fleming

ASHLEY T. BRUNDAGE

Ashley T Brundage (she/her) is the owner of Empowering Differences, a leadership training and public speaking agency. She is a highly sought-after motivational speaker and routinely works with clients on matters of equality and leadership. Through her business, she also specializes in transgender marketing, which empowers businesses to be purposeful in working with trans-owned vendor in their procurement cycles. She has also written her own book, *Empowering Differences*, which teaches people to use their differences to accelerate their career. As a diversity and inclusion leader, Ashley has helped lead Diversity and Inclusion initiatives for a major financial services institution. She is also a member of the GLAAD Board of Directors; the global co-chair of the NGLCC Transgender and Gender Non-Conforming Task Force; a member of the steering committee for Equality Florida's St. Pete Gala; and on the advisory board for Equality Florida's TransAction Florida. To learn more about Ashley and her book visit www.AshleyBrundage.com.

THE PATH TO LIVE

From my childhood, I questioned how things were presented to me. I remember that people would call me by my middle name, Ashley, as a way to pick on me. At the same time, my sister used my middle name as a way to better relate to me. So growing up, having my name used in these two different ways, I knew early on that something wasn't right.

During the 1980s, I didn't know what 'trans' was nor did I have access to any of the resources like what is available on the internet today. I couldn't just look 'trans' up in the encyclopedia and get a full picture of what it meant to be trans. The biggest choice that I made back then was choosing between hand-me-down toys from my brother or my sister. I chose my sister's stuff. As a result, people often ridiculed me for being more feminine, or for standing and walking a certain way. For me, it wasn't a matter of choosing certain things for being more masculine or feminine, it was just what was more comfortable.

As I grew older, I started to realize that I needed to be very, very careful about how I presented and expressed my gender. I learned that there were more social consequences than just being picked on by my brother for the way I acted. Early on, I became more secretive about how I felt and tried to adjust the way I carried myself. By the time I reached my teenage years, the internet was just starting out as a dial-up connection. It wasn't much, but it offered the first chance to dig deeper and find more information about what I had been feeling for so long.

At the time, the terminology was 'transsexual' and early online resources and definitions were not as helpful as what's online today. There was no trans representation on the internet except as a punch line, or as sex workers or porn stars. I didn't see myself as any of these, but I continued to dig deeper into what it meant to be trans. I came across a couple of groups online, made up of wives supporting their husbands who cross-dressed to fill their need to express their femininity. I didn't fit into that group either, but there wasn't an alternative.

Then I started to go into puberty. That's when it got really rough. It was incredibly difficult to see my body becoming more masculine. One day, I was getting to the point where I considered actually walking outside my door as Ashley. I ended up having a conversation with my brother first, telling him what I was planning. He was very blunt with me and said that if I did, I wasn't necessarily going to be alive in a year or have a family to come back to. It wasn't said in a way to put down how I was feeling or what I was going through, it was just the truth.

In all honesty, my brother was right, and him saying that probably saved my life. I can't imagine where I would be, or if I would even be alive at all, if I went through with my plan back then. It was at that point that I decided to lock that part of me away; I latched onto my high school girlfriend Whitney, and we decided to be together. For the next ten years, I did a really good job of hiding the trans part of me and pretended to be male.

During this time, I ended up having kids and they helped me get through this point in my life. Anytime I thought, *I can't continue to live like this* or *I can't keep going*, I would remember that I never wanted to leave them. I could never leave my kids with only one parent, and as a result, my love for them helped me survive those ten years.

In the late 2000s, I ended up losing my job, which was its own blessing, because it enabled me to be a stay-at-home parent. It opened up a lot of time, allowing me to dig deep and find the truth about myself. I still couldn't articulate what

I was feeling or put the proper words behind it. I didn't know the words 'gender dysphoria' or 'transgender,'let alone how to use those words into a sentence. I was practicing avoidance-behavior, which caused problems in my relationship with Whitney. In truth, I wasn't being completely honest with her about what I was going through, and it put a strain on our relationship for a number of years, mostly because I didn't know the whole scope of what I was going through and didn't know how to encapsulate what needed to be said in words.

By 2008 or 2009, there was a lot more information available on transgender people, enough that I could get a clearer understanding of what it even meant to be trans. I started to learn more through internet research and forums, which helped me explain what I'd been feeling for so long. Even with the information, I still wanted multiple perspectives from different counselors before making any decision—I wanted to make sure that this was who I was. I saw several different types of mental health counselors, including one for marriage, one religious/faith-based counselor, an LGBTQ+ specific counselor, and a trans counselor. I went to counselors in multiple states; I wanted to get out of the bubble that I was in and get the perspective that comes with living in different areas. I wanted to get all of their perspectives about the decision that I was thinking of making: to start living authentically.

THE WAY FORWARD

Getting the results from multiple counselors allowed me to embrace that I was a transgender woman, finally giving me the words to describe the heartache and turmoil that I'd felt my whole life. It was a relief to tell Whitney about my gender dysphoria. By this point, the damage had already been done, and all we could do was figure out how to move forward. She accepted me for who I was but we were at a crossroads: could we coexist, not only as partners but also as parents?

Whitney began going with me to the counseling sessions, and though it didn't initially help, it did long-term. Everything at the start was very raw and real, and we had to figure out where we would go from there. We decided it'd be best to spend time apart from one another and that I should stay with my mom. However, before I moved in, I had to come out to my mom and explain what was happening. My mother was distraught for nearly two weeks, thinking maybe she did something wrong or that there was something that she could've done to change me. She was only focused on the wrong points, or why this happened and what "made me this way," as opposed to how to support me going forward. She might've persisted, but my sister came to my defense and stood up for me, saying that my mother needed to support me now more than ever. Gradually, my mother's focus shifted to trying her best to be there and support me, and with time, she came to accept me. Thankfully, she only needed about two weeks to come around and accept me, which was incredibly meaningful.

Our plan was to separate for about three months. On our first night separated, after almost 13 years of being together, Whitney called me crying and asked me to move back home. I considered it, but I thought that we needed to make sure that we were going to be able to work together and really have each other's back before I ran home. Plus, I had to consider how traumatic it would be on our kids if, two weeks later, we realized things didn't work and I moved out again.

We stuck to the plan and maintained a physical distance between us. Gradually, we began to go on weekly dates to see if we could coexist in society together as women. We rebuilt our connection, while trying to adapt and find the next step, which included figuring out how to tell our kids that one of their parents was trans and was going to present as a woman.

Our kids were about five and three years old at the time. Since my oldest was very advanced for his age, we decided to give him the book, *My Princess Boy*. It's about a boy that goes to play at the school playground. Sometimes he wears jeans and other times he wears dresses. So Whitney and I ordered it, and when it arrived, my oldest was super excited to see what was inside.

When he opened it, he was like, "I'm not reading that pink book."

We both said, "Oh no, that's exactly why you're reading it."

Once he was finished reading it, we asked him what the moral of the story was.

He responded, "If you have a friend, you know, they're your friend. No matter what they wear to the playground." He added, "You don't judge a book by its cover. You get to know the person, and then you can decide whether or not you like them."

We were both surprised at how well he grasped it and asked, "What would you say if your dad was dressing like a princess?"

And he was like, "Nah, that would never happen."

I showed him a picture of me, as me, as Ashley, and he was like, "Oh wow, Daddy's very pretty."

RATHER THAN ALLOW MY DIFFERENCES TO ALIENATE ME, **I USED THEM TO ADVANCE MY CAREER.**

And just like that, he accepted me for who I was.

My youngest, who was only three at the time, was just happy that I was coming home and didn't really understand the concept of gender. Telling them meant I could move back home and we explained to both our kids that when I did, I was going to remain the same person, but that I was going to be wearing feminine clothes. Presenting as myself was its own transition and took some time to adjust, but I was able to start living authentically in my own home.

STARTING FROM SQUARE ONE

Going forward, the last domino for me was finding employment. Since my kids were going into kindergarten, and I wasn't going to be staying at home all day, I needed to not only find work, but a new career. I went out to apply at tons of different places but given the recession, I found the process difficult, even without the added hurdles of being trans. After several weeks, I learned quickly I was also going to have to start at the bottom.

At the same time, I had just started presenting as me; no hormone therapy yet, only a wig and some makeup. I also hadn't yet changed my name, so I wrote it as T. Ashley Brundage, trying to get myself into the interview room—but that was only the half of it. Those first few weeks, I must've interviewed for at least forty different jobs. For me, it was one of the darker periods of my life, especially when I was getting laughed at—daily—and told "We would never hire anyone like you." Employers threatened to call the cops on me or accused me of trespassing, which was absolutely crazy. One employer actually had me physically removed from the building.

There was one employer, however, that I had been emailing who had said they didn't care that I was trans. In my head I thought, *Maybe this place could be a good fit*, and since I was more than qualified, it checked off a lot of boxes, enough to let my guard down in hopes that everything would work out. Then came the fine print, where they asked me to pay them about $900 for a certification so I could get the job. Believe it or not, despite not having the money, I was excited about the possibility of getting hired and ended up borrowing the money from a friend. In the end—yep, as you guessed, I was scammed. But that's what happens when you have no hope. If I'd been thinking normally, or even strategically, I would've been suspicious. Hundreds of rejections made it easy to believe this was the light at the end of the tunnel. Now I was out $900 and in debt to my friend. I put my guard back up to make sure it never happened again.

After enduring many months of failed job searches, I finally got my foot in the door as a part-time bank teller. It was exactly what I needed to put my life on the right track. It was such a euphoric moment, finally finding a place that would hire me.

On my first day, they were showing the ropes to a group of new hires, and, coincidentally enough, I wasn't the only trans person at the training. There was a trans man there and I was blown away—like, what are the chances that this company not only hired me, but also made it so I went through training with another trans person? I didn't know then that this new experience would later shape my life on the path to becoming a diversity and inclusion educator, so that no other trans or LGBTQ+ person would have to go through the professional humiliation I'd gone through.

WORKING UP THE CORPORATE LADDER

Starting on the ground floor as a part-time bank teller, I worked hard to advance my career. I made sure that my boss and immediate supervisor noticed my efforts. I took small actions every week that I could control, like showing up early to work, working efficiently, and becoming a top performer. All of these were in my control, and in a short amount of time, I moved from part-time teller to full-time, and was soon talking with my boss about being a manager.

It was around this time that I started developing my career, from commercial bank to business banking to investment licenses, all with active engagement in communities as key drivers in my success in business. This was over the course of three years. I was active in multiple LGBTQ+ networking communities, and was purposeful to have revenue tied to community engagement. I put together a business plan to track results from community engagements through diversity and inclusion. For example, when I was serving on the board as the president of the Tampa Bay LGBTQ+ Chamber of Commerce, I was meeting a lot of business owners, which helped me to drive revenue to the bank. As my deals were getting the nod, I made sure the work I was doing and the business that I was driving to the bank was getting noticed, especially since I could get a whole year's worth of new clients from one weekend of networking.

I was also purposefully going beyond the safe walls of the communities where I knew I would be recognized and accepted. I went to women's community events and multicultural events, and I made sure that I had an explicit purpose in going there, whether it was to network and get my name out in these communities, or to advertise and drive more business to the bank. I used my time wisely and positioned myself to get my name noticed at the bank and in the world-at-large. I made sure that I was standing out, but not sticking out. I did this by being a voice of reason for business—you wouldn't necessarily expect a six-foot-tall trans woman to come at you, prepared and strategic in what she talks about. But I rose to the occasion, and walked into those meeting rooms with statistics and research about LGBTQ+ people and the benefits of having more diversity in the workplace. In the end, the hard work paid off and led me to the multiple positions that I now hold in the community. Rather than allow my differences to alienate me, I used them to advance my career.

Since I brought these new ideas to the table and was able to fit into these circles, talking about business or strategic growth—or even sports—I stood out in the higher-ups' minds. It was a matter of putting myself in the right positions at the right times. For example, I was at an award ceremony for the company and instead of doing what I wanted to do during our downtime, which was shopping, I put myself in the shoes of the CEO and thought about what he would be doing right now, which was golfing. So I went to the golf course and looked around for the CEO. Where was the head of corporate banking? I found several members of the inner circle golfing together. It was tempting to up and leave, but I was already committed; I wanted to change my perspective and be more purposeful, deciding instead to hop right over to the three other bankers from my branch. By the end of the day, I got to know them quite well. Months later, I got a phone call from my CEO, telling me that I was going to be inducted into the employee hall of fame and winning the bank award. I later learned one of the people that I'd played golf with that day was on the voting board.

The more I put myself out there and owned who I was, the more good luck I had. Soon, I got to have dinner with the CEO, lunch with the full C-suite of executives, and even gave a livestream address to the entire company. Three months later, I met with the executives and positioned myself with the Chief Diversity Officer and the CEO to create the role that I now have, as the VP of Diversity and Inclusion with the bank. It wasn't the way that I had anticipated meeting the CEO and the other executives but it was my foot in the door. By being purposeful in getting people to advocate for me, I was able to have a panel of people come to my support when the award came up and it returned positive dividends in helping me get my current position.

As I was moving up through the bank, I was also being asked to share my story very often. During the former months of job searching, I regularly had to educate others on equality, leadership, and transgender people. It led me to see myself as an educator on equality and leadership, because those are the two things that I talk most about. That was how I eventually stepped into creating a business to formalize what I was doing already. This was the start of Empowering Differences. Since then, I've continued to grow my speaking business, teaching a wide variety of audiences about equality and leadership. Through doing this work and starting my own business I've written my book, *Empowering Differences*, in which I teach people how to use their differences to advance their careers and how to uplift those around them. I go more in depth into my story, personal struggles, and how I've overcome them.

THE COST OF TRANSITION

Success didn't come without its trials. While rising through the ranks at the bank, I was also trying to save up as much as I could for the costs of transitioning, while at the same time providing for my family. My kids were getting older, and I had to be there to care for them. Starting part-time and working hard to pay the bills amid a nationally rising cost of living, it took me five years to officially change my name and gradually begin to medically transition.

Just getting a name change can cost upwards of $400, which is why it took me so long to do. At the same time, I also had to save for the transition-related medical bills that I knew would be coming, which took a serious financial toll on me, as it does most trans people. In order to even see a physician about starting hormones, you have to see a therapist so they can diagnose you with gender dysphoria. It usually takes multiple sessions, until they give you a letter saying that hormone replacement therapy (HRT) is medically necessary. Then you have to find a doctor who will actually prescribe you hormones, which means more time and money for more visits.

Once prescribed hormones, I was faced with having to pay for HRT and the many blood tests involved increasing your dosage. This is all before even considering the cost of surgeries: top surgery, gender confirmation surgery, and facial feminization surgery. How I ended up being able to pay for my gender confirmation surgery was actually by pure chance.

At the beginning of 2018, I was driving to Orlando when someone rear-ended my car. It wasn't a serious car crash, but afterward I felt this terrible pain in my stomach. Going to the hospital several days later, I found out that my appendix was ruptured and I almost died because of it. Surprisingly, the good side of this happening was that I ended up reaching my annual out-of-pocket maximum for my insurance, so now every other medical procedure that year would be completely covered. And as luck would have it, I was able to make an appointment and have gender confirmation surgery by the end of the year.

Looking back at everything, I know I wouldn't have waited five years to start medically transitioning, but rather I would have forced myself to find a way to make it possible: it would have been five fewer years of having testosterone running through my body. That would have been five more years of my life that I could have felt so much more comfortable in my own skin.

REPRESENTATION MATTERS

Being in the place and the position that I am today, I'd say that my life is certainly a lot better than where I used to be. I've had a lot of people come up to me, after sharing my story, and say things like, "Ashley, you have such a fabulous life!" and I just say, "There's a lot of work that goes into that."

I continue to work all these different avenues and volunteer at many organizations. There's a cost to everything. Attending a conference, well, that's time that I'm not with my kids; it's a constant give and take. Nothing was ever handed to me; I worked for everything, and then some—above and beyond what a non-trans person has to do. That's something I wish I could tell my younger self: you have to realize that you'll have to work so much harder than people who are cisgender. Getting your foot in the door is only a fraction of the ladder that you have to climb, and trying to get up that ladder is hard.

And if you mess something up, you aren't just the girl who messed up, you're the *trans* girl who messed up. Having that weight of representing a community of people is not something I asked for, but it's how people perceive me. We're never judged just as a person but always as a trans person. That's a cruel reality for any minority group.

It's also important to share our stories, to show that we are more than just a label or a standard medical model. We each have our own lives and history that led us to be the people we are today.

If there's one take-away from my story, let it be how important it is for trans and nonbinary people to have support. My family literally saved my life and are the reason I'm here today. Having someone supportive—like my wife—through the trials of what I went through also saved my life. There were times I'd invite family members to a really important speech and they wouldn't come, but Whitney was there each and every time. Having at least one person there in my corner meant the world to me and pushed me to keep going, driving change for myself and the community.

We all have an opportunity to make a difference in (and potentially save) someone else's life. It could be your coworker—anyone—and you have a responsibility to help them. It's as easy as saying, "How're you doing today?" or "What can I do to help you out?" It's not a huge commitment to be compassionate and understanding of someone's situation. Being supportive doesn't mean that you have to go through transition as well or have to be completely immersed in a person's life; it's just caring about another person. Small things matter. You never know what's happening inside someone else's mind or what they're going through. So don't underestimate that it could be you who supports another person's life and dream.

IF THERE'S ONE TAKE-AWAY FROM MY STORY, LET IT BE **HOW IMPORTANT IT IS FOR TRANS AND NONBINARY PEOPLE TO HAVE SUPPORT.** MY FAMILY LITERALLY SAVED MY LIFE AND ARE THE REASON I'M HERE TODAY.

Words of advice to trans or nonbinary people: don't share your story or speak your truth for free. If you are working for a company that wants to showcase its support at Pride or are looking for a trans speaker for the event, don't speak for free. It's exciting, saying that you spoke at the event or in front of hundreds of people, but the reality is that too often companies will pay other speakers but not LGBTQ+ speakers. Even if they do pay, it's usually less than they would for those who are speaking on leadership, careers, etc. Of course, I'm not saying go to your LGBTQ+ community center and tell them that you want them to pay you to speak, but if a million-dollar organization wants you to share something about your experience, and they might use it as marketing, you need to make sure you're protecting not only your own voice, but all of our voices.

The concern lies in the fact that all too often companies that have had a history of discriminating and treating their LGBTQ+ workers terribly, turn around when June hits, making their logo a rainbow, and pretend to be an 'ally' for the community just for that month. This is why, regardless of whether you are cis, trans, or nonbinary, we all should be mindful of who we are investing in and where we are spending our money. We should all be really purposeful to spend our money with businesses that support equality and diversity for all—all the time, not just supporting for one month in the summer. Representation matters, and we need to actively invest in supporting businesses and companies that are actively providing a platform for LGBTQ+ leaders. Not just for the businesses, but for the communities and lives impacted. I choose to share my story to showcase that I'm a visible leader. Thinking about access to information, how important it is, and how accessible it is now, I wanted to continue to be part of it. There are plenty of trans kids in schools that need positive role models showcasing trans excellence. You can be your authentic self while rising to leadership positions. You can be the CEO of a company or run your own business, or even be the VP of Diversity and Inclusion for a major services organization. If you can dream it, you can be it.

Ashley T. Brundage

RHODES PERRY

Rhodes Perry (he/him) is the founder and CEO of Rhodes Perry Consulting (RPC) and best-selling author of *Belonging at Work*. His firm works with leaders, visionaries, and change agents to build belonging and help organizations reach industry breakthroughs. A life-long human rights advocate, Rhodes has been instrumental in championing policy changes and new laws nationwide to protect the LGBTQI+ communities. His podcast, *The Out Entrepreneur*, features interviews with LGBTQI+ entrepreneurs about their experiences in the workplace.

WAITING FOR A CHANCE TO EXPLORE

Growing up, I ran around and played games with my older brother. Early on, as soon as I could understand gender, I thought of myself as his younger brother, not his sister. No one in my family corrected my understanding of my gender until around five or six, when I started getting called a 'tomboy.' For a time, being a tomboy was cute, but by the time I reached twelve years old, it stopped being cute and became a form of what I call 'gender jail' (though I didn't have a word for it at the time). As I experienced social pressure to perform femininity, tomboy felt like a put-down.

"You're a girl, okay," my family would say. "You need to behave like a young girl behaves."

A complicating wrinkle to my childhood: I grew up Catholic in the South, which meant I faced huge pressure to conform and be more "traditionally" feminine.

At a young age, getting mixed messages about how I needed to perform my gender in the world was really challenging, but subconsciously I knew in order to survive in this environment, I had to play by rules that felt inauthentic to who I really am. As time passed, I went from living as a carefree 'tomboy' to following all the gender rules that other people laid out for me. There was nothing I wanted more than to get out of the South and live my life, so I endured it all, striving to do well in school and in sports to make that a reality.

Throughout high school, I found an outlet through being on the cross-country, track, basketball, and softball teams. I felt more like myself wearing the track and basketball outfits since they were fairly androgynous. Playing sports in high school served as a lifeline for me. I knew that there was something significant about why I felt more comfortable playing sports and wearing clothing that aligned more with my true gender. At the time, I had no way to explain how I felt; I just knew I didn't fit in with anyone around me. My plan was to be an exceptional student athlete in order to get out of Florida and experience the world.

Fitting in and getting along with others were two different things. I easily connected with the honors & AP students, just as effortlessly as I related to the jocks, goth kids, and so many other students from different walks of life. I was very adaptive—it was a survival skill that I refined throughout high school that helped me endure this challenging time. In hindsight, if I had remained isolated in the small town I grew up in, and hadn't adapted to get along, then I don't know where I'd be right now—or if I'd even be here. As trans folks, that's how we survive in a world that wasn't entirely built for us—or rather, the world is built for us, but it has in it a binary culture that can't deal with anything other than zeros and ones.

After high school, I went to the University of Notre Dame, a private Catholic college in South Bend, Indiana. As a Catholic kid, I knew that this great school would please my parents, and be my ticket out of Florida. I had the added incentive of earning a Naval ROTC scholarship, which paid for me to go to college while I was training to be a Naval Officer. Accepting this scholarship had one caveat—after I completed my under-graduate degree, I'd have to serve in the Navy for four years. This was in 1998, a time of "peace" prior to 9/11 and the wars in Iraq and Afghanistan. This opportunity was a great way to attend college, since my family lacked the resources to fund my education. Going to Notre Dame allowed me to escape the South—South Bend was the first stop on my world tour.

STARTING TO LEARN WHO I AM

During my first year of college, I was ranked the top of my class out of all the men and women participating in the Naval ROTC program. This was a really big deal, as it would allow me to have top picks of the career assignment I would earn upon graduation. My commanding officer was push-ing me to consider becoming a pilot, as they wanted more women to enroll in the program.

At the end of the first year, we were called individually to take oral exams. Each cadet had to go into the office alone and sit at this huge, mahogany table across from military brass on all sides of the table.

I remember this very clearly: A Marine officer was sitting next to one of the commanders who asked me, "Midshipman Perry, do you know the military's stance on lesbians and gays?"

I was taken aback and confused. *Why would he ask that question? Why did it even matter?* Sadly, I did know about the military's 'Don't Ask; Don't Tell' policy, and when I said so, we moved on to the next item. After leaving the room, I couldn't get it out of my head. I had never experienced that specific kind of targeting before. At the time, my gender expression was fairly feminine and I simply didn't have time to think about dating. I felt targeted, and in hindsight, I *was* targeted. I believe that the Marine who asked this question resented that I was outperforming people of all genders in my class. The question stung me.

After my oral exams, I was left with one of the hardest choices of my young life. After my first year of college, the scholar-ship gave each cadet a choice: 1) continue with the ROTC program and commit to four years of military service after graduation, or 2) exit the program with your first year of college paid, but then the rest of the three-year tuition is up for you to cover. In the end, I was committed to completing my studies in Economics and Gender Studies, and knew that the military wasn't the right place for me. I had to get resourceful to find ways to pay for college, and I knew the ROTC scholarship was no longer an option. In hindsight, had I continued with the ROTC program, I worry that my mental health and overall well-being would have been jeopardized. I'm grateful I had the foresight and good judgement to make such a big decision with significant consequences.

GETTING MIXED MESSAGES ABOUT HOW I NEEDED TO PERFORM MY GENDER IN THE WORLD WAS REALLY CHALLENGING, BUT **SUBCONSCIOUSLY I KNEW IN ORDER TO SURVIVE IN THIS ENVIRONMENT, I HAD TO PLAY BY RULES THAT FELT INAUTHENTIC** TO WHO I REALLY AM.

By sophomore year, I had not forgotten about that Marine Officer's question. *Why me? What about me made him ask that?* Taking stock of my early life, I remember my best friend asking if I was a lesbian when I was fourteen. Even my mom questioned my sexual orientation back then too. Up until this point in my life, I wasn't interested in the idea of dating. As I began looking inward to better understand myself and my sexual orientation, I was fortunate to have a number of LGBTQ+ people in my life. One of whom invited me to a LGBTQ+ event as an ally, which felt like such a big step in my coming out journey.

As I entered through the doorway in the building where the meeting was held, I felt a sense of clarity, purpose, and even a degree of magic. There, I bore witness to a vibrant community of my fellow classmates—not only thriving, but demanding changes to improve the lives and well-being of students, faculty, and staff at the University. Being in such close proximity to so many LGBTQ+ people was a wake-up call that I was a part of this community, and it gave me hope and confidence that everything would be okay.

The campus student LGBTQ+ group, OUTreachND, was created for two primary reasons. The first was to offer peer support and education, to help a group of largely Catholic kids reconcile their faith with the reality of who they were. This support aspect of the group helped each of us find a source of pride in our identities and to find strength to continue living with a greater sense of authenticity. The second reason why the group existed was to advocate for the fair treatment and full inclusion of LGBTQ+ students, faculty, and staff. At the time, we were urging the University to include nondis-crimination protections for LGBTQ+ campus stakeholders; for student affairs to recognize and fund our student grou,p(like all other student run organizations on campus; and to ban conversion therapy groups like Exodus International from speaking on our campus, causing further harm to young people coming to terms with their sexual orientation and gender identity.

During my first meeting, the President of OUTreachND spoke passionately to us about her own coming out story, her parents' allyship journey, and also the reason why she was organizing a hunger strike: to demand that the University's administration update the campus' nondiscrimination policy. Her commitment to making the University more inclusive was impressive and her energy was magnetic—she was a natural leader. The following week, to show the administration they needed to acknowledge our request to have nondiscrimination policies and recognize us as part of the school's community, the hunger strike began.

When the woman who was speaking ended up being my first girlfriend, I thought, *Okay, cool, now I'm a lesbian.* Unlike the word 'tomboy,' this felt like a better way of describing myself—it helped me describe a core aspect of my social identity. After the semester ended, I went home and I wrote this super long coming out letter to my parents—works cited and everything—explaining what it meant to be a lesbian and giving them a ton of different resources and groups for parental support, including Parents and Friends of Lesbians and Gays (PFLAG).

Before giving my parents the letter, I drove to my girlfriend's house, three hours away, where I was welcomed by her Catholic PFLAG parents. They gave me a ton of support and even offered to talk to my parents in the event they didn't take the news well. I was super thankful that when I went back to see my parents, I wasn't kicked out or disowned, even though there was a lot of crying.

The first thing my mom said was, "We love you no matter what," and that was a relief to hear.

But my dad's response left a scar. After 20 years of reflection, I know the intent behind his fear response was to protect me, yet the impact was quite the opposite.

His words and actions fractured our relationship. I felt like I'd lost not only a parent but my best friend. It took many years and a lot of patience on both our parts to repair it. Thankfully my girlfriend's mom buffered the initial fury. She drove to my parents' house and they spent a full day together, making connections and gaining new understandings of themselves and our world. The peer-to-peer connection helped my parents realize, if they didn't commit to learning more about me and LGBTQ+ communities, then they weren't going to have a relationship with me.

Before I left for my junior year of college, I let them know that I didn't want to come back to Florida, unless they were willing to continue learning and commit to respecting me and those in my community. Over time, they took small steps towards greater understanding, because they deeply loved me and wanted me in their lives.

THE CORE OF MY IDENTITY

During my junior year at Notre Dame, I traveled with OUTreachND students to Chicago for one of the nation's largest LGBTQ+ conferences, Creating Change. As I listened to the brilliant Urvashi Vaid talk about the state of LGBTQ+ civil and human rights, I admired how she connected with and inspired her audience. She shared her long-term vision of where the movement and the community needed to go, with more of us finding our voices and advocating for change. At the time, the US lacked basic LGBTQ+ civil and human rights. Many advocacy organizations focused resources on holding government and business communities accountable to addressing the HIV/AIDS epidemic. As Urvashi spoke, it was there, at 19 years old, that I committed to being a part of this change, even though at the time I wasn't quite sure where I fit in this picture.

As each semester passed, I was working towards getting more comfortable with my queer self. By junior year, my gender identity came to the forefront, with an especially renewed focus on trans men like Brandon Teena because of the Oscar-winning 1999 film, *Boys Don't Cry*, which was all over the news cycles. Sadly, this film was some of the only media featuring a trans person. That is, aside from the daytime TV shows of the time, which sensationalized the lives and lived experiences of trans people, or even more alarmingly, late-night comedy skits and films, like *Ace Ventura*, where a person's gender identity or expression was a punch line. Bottom line, there was a significant lack of media that depicted anything positive about trans people.

For me, Brandon Teena was the only trans masculine person that I had access to. I learned of his story from the film, and the supplemental profiles about his life. When I first saw pictures of him as a child, everything felt like it stopped. He looked really similar to me. I looked into his eyes and I just saw myself in that picture and thought, *Oh my god; he's just like me!* Reading about how his life was taken from him (because he was trans) terrified me, and like most things that scare me, I became curious as to why it so badly scared me—I wanted to put the pieces together and gain greater clarity.

Between my junior and senior years of college, I earned a scholarship for a summer internship in Washington,

DC, working as a communications intern for the National Organization of Women (NOW). During that time, our communications team facilitated conversations about feminism, gender identity, and the women's rights movement. While the organization moved to include transgender women in its mission in the late 1990s, a small faction of the organization's members was unhappy with this move, and used the 2001 National Convention as a place to raise these concerns, as members were convening from around the country to vote for NOW's next President. I played a small role in influencing some members in understanding why trans women were women, and why the organization had enough room for both transgender and cisgender women. As I bore witness to members fumbling towards understanding transgender people, I gained greater confidence in my understanding of trans identities, and my role as an advocate.

When it came time to vote, the majority of members pledged to honor the organization's commitment to advocate for all women, transgender and cisgender alike. It was a move that gave greater voice and visibility to the transgender women of the organization, and to the greater movement for transgender rights taking root in the country. Being part of this experience gave me a lot of courage to be myself, and encouraged me to continue refining my skills as an advocate for social and economic justice.

COMING INTO MY OWN

Returning for my senior year at Notre Dame, I knew there was something more to my gender I needed to explore, and yet, I also knew I was returning to a school where survival as a queer student was the first and only priority. On campus, the dorms were (and are still) segregated by gender. In 2001, the thought of being the first ND student to openly transition was inconceivable. Given the University lacked a basic nondiscrimination policy, pushing for a gender inclusive housing policy would surely make things far more complicated than I could handle as I began to plot what to do next, post-graduation.

After graduation, I landed my first job as an honors paralegal working for the Department of Justice in Washington, DC. It was in this first year living alone in a relatively LGBTQ+ friendly city where I began to explore my gender through performing in the DC Drag King troupe. While some found community, relationships, and connection through drag performance, I found myself. With each show, I had the chance to perform a different shade of masculinity...from the more butch presentations of Bruce Springsteen and Frank Sinatra, to the more androgynous presentations of David Bowie or Mick Jagger, I had the chance to play. In this community of fellow gender benders, I had my first chance to test out what it would feel like to socially transition, my first chance to use a different name from my legal name, and try on gender neutral and male pronouns.

On March 8, International Women's Day, I first came out to my friend group. I gathered everyone together, and told them I was a trans man, and that I was there as a feminist and an ally for gender justice. It was such a powerful moment for me because everyone was like, "We love and support you!" My longtime friends and my partner at the time were the first people I told. For them, it made a lot of sense, even if it meant getting used to the new name and pronouns. Basically, they were on team Rhodes from day one and that felt pretty awesome, having their support. My next thought was, *Who else would be safe to tell?*

THERE WAS NO RIGHT
OR WRONG WAY TO
START, BUT **THE
IMPORTANT THING
IS THAT YOU START
SOMEWHERE.**

The cool thing about the early part of transitioning was how easy it was with random strangers. Meeting me for the first time, they only met me as Rhodes, so they had no reason to trip up on my name or pronouns. It was gratifying for them to get my name and pronouns correct right from the beginning. Within a short period of time, I got very resourceful and figured out how to safely socially, legally, and medically transition and really started to feel good about myself.

While moving into my role as a feminist trans man engaged in allyship work, I felt empowered, but I also recognized the loss of losing insider access to the powerful spaces women (both transgender and cisgender) create. So much of what had made me 'me' was the confidence that I got from these kinds of women-centered spaces. Once I was on the outside, as a guy engaged in feminist allyship work, I had to look at things from an entirely new perspective. I wanted to find a way of employing my newfound privilege to drop ladders down for women, nonbinary, and gender diverse people in a way that would have a positive impact on the world.

Now 22, I was well on my way and coming into my own. I had socially transitioned within my friend group, and legally changed my name, which allowed my co-workers to use my new name and pronouns as well. The biggest hurdle at the time was returning to Florida to share the news with my family. Three months after I started hormone therapy treatment, my voice started changing enough that I sounded like I had a permanent cold.

When my parents picked me up from the airport, my mom kept asking me, "Honey, are you okay? You sound like you have a bad cold."

My mom has great intuition and could tell I wasn't being forthright, and pressed me to explain what was going on.

It was then, driving in the car, that I offered a crash course into what it meant to be transgender, and that I was a transgender guy.

A few years of knowledge about LGBTQ+ communities didn't prepare my parents for what they were just learning about their...son. While they fumbled with how to respond, they did have some resiliency skills to draw upon because they had already navigated the initial coming out with regards to my sexual orientation. Given that experience, there was a pathway that they could follow. *Our kid is telling us something about them that is important. We don't understand it but we've been here before.* Also given that there weren't many positive trans stories at the time period I came out to them, they were also probably thinking, *Okay, we love our kid, but what will his life be like now?* Especially since I was scheduled to get top surgery in less than two weeks.

Even though they had a road map to follow, it still took them years to fully come to terms with what it means for them to have a trans son, and what it means for me to be a trans man. In the beginning, it seemed like they would never get my name or pronouns right. But while I had years to accept myself, I recognize now that I was expecting them to immediately understand, respect, and affirm me with no notice. I was impatient with their learning curve, and I let them know I wanted them to be a part of my life, but I also didn't want to be traumatized every time they misgendered me, especially when it happened in public. I knew that this was who I was, and I felt like, *You're either on team Rhodes, or you're an obstacle in the way for me to live a fully authentic version of my life.* The fumbling and repair work I was committed to engaging in with my family helped us strengthen our adult relationships, and their unconditional love gave me strength to move forward with my transition. This love is something I don't for a second take for granted, recognizing that so many of my friends and trans family weren't as fortunate.

CHANGING THE NARRATIVE

Working for a LGBTQ+ organization, I found there was so much transphobia present within some of these organizations. At the time, the 'T' in LGBTQ+ was silent, and was included more for marketing to draw support from the trans community, rather than include it. I saw the in-fighting firsthand and questioned what I was worth to the movement. In other words, if they couldn't get it right, then who would? Especially without having to play 20 questions about my body and my identity. At the time, I felt like my parents would forever struggle to understand me, while the largely cisgender gay and lesbian leaders within the LGBTQ+ community failed to demonstrate respect and support for transgender people like me.

I couldn't imagine a world—or even a group of people—that would get it. Where were the queer cisgender folks putting their allyship into action? Everywhere in the community I went, it seemed like I had to explain myself again and again, only to be met with more resistance and questions about my body or identity. Early lesbian and gay organizations introduced and advocated for laws that only protected against discrimination on the basis of sexual orientation and didn't include gender identity, which ultimately excluded transgender and nonbinary folks. Since I'd worked at several LGBTQ+ nonprofits throughout my early career, as well as the US Justice Department and the White House, I was often asked to be the one to do presentations on how to be more trans-inclusive. This was often the case for LGBTQ+

organizations that allegedly provided affirming services to transgender people.

With the dawn of the Obama Presidency in 2008, a new era of business leaders began embracing the principles of LGBTQ+ diversity, equity, and inclusion. Even Congress and federal agencies were starting their own journeys to expand their nondiscrimination policies and workforce trainings to gain a greater understanding of LGBTQ+ workers, transgender and nonbinary stakeholders in particular. At this time, I was working at PFLAG National, where I helped establish their federal policy agenda, pushing for Title IX protections to include LGBTQ+ students, urging Congress to pass the Employment Nondiscrimination Act, and pressing the Department of Health and Human Services to ensure Affordable Healthcare Act protections for LGBTQ+ patients.

Wherever it was needed, I was brought in to do some kind of organizational change or capacity building project, whether that was rewriting internal healthcare policies for transgender employees or creating the groundwork for more trans-inclusive employee practices. I ended up moving to New York City to advise the City's government around implementing policy protections and improving practices for LGBTQ+ young people involved in foster care and juvenile justice settings. It was groundbreaking work, but the reality in 2012 was that there was still resistance to investing in the proven strategies that would allow the City's agencies' cultures to catch up with existing laws and policies.

Leading up the City's Office of LGBTQ+ Policy and Practice, we secured a number of successes that began to gain national attention from other larger municipalities looking to adopt our approach. Initially, I began offering as much technical support to these municipalities as I could, yet I never had enough time to offer the necessary coaching, resources and expertise that their work required. Over time, I realized that my experience, talents, and innovative approach could be a real asset to the growing number of government agencies and businesses who were trying to build gender inclusive workplaces.

In 2015, I took the entrepreneurial leap and started my own consulting and coaching firm to help these executives build a greater sense of psychological safety, trust, and belonging for underrepresented folks—including trans-gender and nonbinary people—who are the least likely to feel safe on the job.

This was when I began Rhodes Perry Consulting and started writing my best-selling book, *Belonging at Work*. Initially, I focused the practice on building LGBTQ-affirming diverse, equitable, and inclusive workplaces, and began coaching executives on how embracing inclusive leadership prac-tices can help them welcome and respect their LGBTQ+ staff. My firm helped these leaders articulate, prioritize, and implement their DEI commitments and values into everyday practices. This focus was my entry point into the DEI consulting field. Given my past successes working with government agencies in New York City, my business earned government contracts to offer similar strategy, capacity building, and executive coaching. Today, my work has evolved to be about inclusive leadership development and managing organizational change, with the goal of helping leaders build a greater sense of belonging at work for all stakeholders.

Today, with a large social platform, I uplift the voices of other LGBTQ+ entrepreneurs through my podcast, *The Out Entrepreneur*. Each episode, I interview LGBTQ+

entrepreneurs about their journey and experiences in business, and ask if they have any advice to share with other leaders and aspiring entrepreneurs. It took 15 years to take the leap in starting my own business. Although I didn't start out with the intention of being an out entrepreneur, I always knew this was the direction I wanted to go. I believe that's how you evolve as a business leader: you have an idea, and that idea gets refined as you continue to blend your skills into the thing that you want to do, the thing that inspires you to jump out of bed each day. There was no right or wrong way to start, but the important thing is that you start somewhere.

Navigating my gender transition early in my life, and doing the type of advocacy and change management work that I've engaged in over the past two decades, has given me a renewed sense of clarity as to why I continue to build a business that helps leaders, visionaries, and change agents build a better world. It also helps me understand the very real people and communities that I want to positively impact and uplift.

WHERE WE GO FROM HERE

My life has been a wild ride. Through my gender transition, I've gained so much clarity and confidence in who I am as a person. It's also helped me put everything into perspective. For example, if I'm going through something difficult, and it feels like I'm not sure where to go, I remember that we're all making this up as we go along. Nothing in my life has been as hard as figuring out my gender transition, socially, legally, and medically. There isn't necessarily any one way to do it; there's not a manual saying, "Here you go, good luck transitioning!" Starting my business, I thought, *Oh my god, how am*

I going to do this? And then I realized, *Well, I've figured out transitioning genders, so I should be able to figure this one out too.* Even though there are business building roadmaps out there, I can build my business my own way and follow the path that feels most authentic to me.

Through my journey, I learned that many cisgender people focus on the medical side of transition. They want to know everything about it, as if we figure this part out first, and then—BOOM—there we are. We are more than just the medical model of transition and our identities are more than just our transness or whether or not we've had "the surgery." That's only a part of our journeys, and we are all trying to figure this out as we go. It's the social transition that's forever ongoing. In my experience, it was figuring out how to navigate the world and where I fit in, or if I even fit in at all. By that I mean I'm constantly scanning each new space I enter, asking myself, *Am I safe, or do I need to make a quick exit?*

This is because I'm largely invisible.

When I meet new folks, they assume I'm a cisgender, white, gay man. In these moments, I'm often wondering, *Can this new group of people handle all of me?* When I meet new people, I want to be authentic, to be myself unapologetically, 100 percent of the time, but because I don't know how they'll react, I hold back and don't bring that side out as much as I'd like to. Beyond fears for my safety, I don't have the time or patience to bring them along and get them to a point where they can understand me, unless I'm getting paid to train them. It takes a great sense of safety and trust to explain that transgender and nonbinary people are more than the hyper-sensationalized stories that are shown in the mass media. We are more than just the medical model of transition and there are so many other pieces that define us other than this one identity. We have so many other stories to share.

My journey is ongoing and will continue to evolve. As I grow as a person, as a business leader, and as a human rights advocate, I will continue to employ my privilege and platform to educate people to create a more inclusive environment and culture, prioritizing those people most likely to feel excluded. It's easy to pat ourselves on the back and say, "Look how far we've come," but the reality is that we have so much more to do in terms of equity, justice, and liberation. There are still so many misconceptions and laws that specifically target LGBTQ+ people and restrict our rights, and I'm committed to correcting the record and making positive changes for my rainbow family and friends.

Advocacy and activism mean something different for everyone. For me, it's doing the work that I'm doing now, creating more inclusive workplace environments and amplifying the voices that aren't being heard. Advocacy doesn't always involve being in the limelight or on the front page. Rather, it can include simple actions like supporting someone going through a gender transition, or by calling out someone who makes a transphobic joke or misgenders someone. There are no small actions when making big cultural changes—in fact small actions are something that can yield positive returns on a community and literally save someone's life.

For any transgender and nonbinary people reading this, my advice is to be the artist of your own life and really listen to yourself. You have to get quiet and listen to your deepest inner self about what it is that you want and who you are. That's about gender but it's also about everything else in your life. However if you are able to listen to that tiny voice inside you—whether that's meditating out in nature or cutting out all the distractions for a moment—that voice will tell you what you need to do and where you want to go.

If you know you're on a gender journey, but you're feeling out of alignment about the direction you're heading, get curious about what that is and trust yourself on what feels right. Follow those breadcrumbs and trust that what you're feeling has a purpose behind it. That was how I felt early on before I knew who I was. I kept following what felt right and eventually found the words to describe what I was feeling. Once you pivot, once you take that first tiny turn towards a new direction, life gets a lot happier.

The transgender journey may not be easy, but it's absolutely worth it. It takes a lot of patience to get to where you want to be, and patience for the people in your life that take a long time to understand what you're going through. I know that was definitely not what I wanted to hear when I first came out. Like, *Are you kidding me? You're still in Trans 101? Catch up to the 501 content today, because that's where I am!* At the time I came out, I'd already had 20 years to figure out my gender and understand the terminology that felt best to describe who I was. It might take time for people to come around and accept you. That's the cruel reality. On the other hand, you need to live your life for you, and know that when you move at the speed of trust with those in your life, the people who stick with you will develop into some of the most meaningful relationships.

In the end—cultivate patience. Trust yourself to make the choices you need to make. Follow the path that you need to walk to make sure that you are living as authentically as you can. Something that I wish I could've told my younger self when I was going through my gender transition, that I can tell you instead, is: I love you. Keep going. The world is amazing and it's going to get better. You're going to make it better.

Rhodes Perry

BROOKE COOPER

Brooke Cooper (she/her) is a mother of two children, working to inspire and offer advice to transgender people, especially trans college students, as they move on from their academic years and enter the workforce. Through her 20 years in the banking industry, she has educated, provided career counseling advice, spoken at conferences and classes, all in hopes of passing along what she's learned through experience, to young trans and nonbinary people. She has recently legally affirmed her identity by changing her gender marker on her identification documents. Due to her job, she has decided to remain anonymous.

GROWING UP WITH EXPECTATIONS

Beginning as young as four years old, I used to color my fingernails with magic markers. By five and six, I used to dress up in heels and put on makeup, playing dress-up and pretending to be a girl. It was a fun "kid thing" that I was doing, as well as the earliest expression of my gender identity. By nine or ten years old, I knew that I was different from the other kids in my neighborhood on an eastern North Carolina military base. Although I knew I was different, I didn't have any language to describe exactly how I felt, other than knowing I didn't feel the same way as the other kids or adults did.

During my teenage years, there were expectations, spoken and unspoken, that constantly determined who I was supposed to be and how I should look and act. At 18, my family put immense pressure on me to enlist in the military. It was the family way, since nearly everyone in my family had also enlisted: my aunt and grandad were career colonels and several others were senior officers as well.

One early struggle to understand my gender identity had to do with the way I wore my hair. Growing up, I had a buzz cut, another expectation imposed by my family; I couldn't stand it. For years, I desperately wanted long hair—I often loved imagining what I'd look like and how it would make me feel. I had to keep this secret because I couldn't let anyone in my family know, nor could I try and grow it out. It was my personal curiosity, and an example of my desire to try feminine things, even though everyone around me was busy trying to fit me into this box of how I should be. As a result, I repressed a lot of the feelings that I'd had from an early age. I knew there would be repercussions and backlash if I tried to follow what I was feeling or acted on what I wanted.

The one thing I knew for certain: I wasn't a guy, no matter how much my family tried to fit me into the box of being one. The only thing I could do was keep everything I felt down. I believed what I wanted could never happen and attempted to defeat the feelings that I did have. I went along with playing football, soccer, and other sports in high school, to make myself feel more masculine, thinking to myself that I was putting down the thoughts and feelings. The thoughts may have dissipated but they never truly went away.

When it came time for me to decide about enlisting in the military, I couldn't. Instead, I chose to go to college. This was during the "Don't Ask, Don't Tell" Clinton administration and I just couldn't reconcile joining the military with who I knew myself to be. There was no leeway: who they would expect me to be would never feel right. Deep down in my heart, I understood that the life and the person I wanted for myself wasn't compatible with their expectations. I decided, difficult as it was, to inform my family and face reality. That was the first step toward asserting the life I wanted, the first major decision that I'd made for myself in terms of how I wanted to live my life. I got a ton of backlash, confusion, and anger from different family members. But I kept going.

Subverting all the expectations put on me—by my family, society, and friends—was by no means an easy decision, but I knew it was the right decision for me; it was what I wanted to do. It was a step in the right direction of putting my needs and wants in the front of my life.

Throughout the years though, I was still battling internal feelings of gender dysphoria and the want to embrace being feminine and be myself100 percent of the time.

For many years, I considered that I was just a cross-dresser, that putting on feminine clothes was just a fun thing to do that felt more comfortable in a way that I didn't understand yet. One of the first times I really felt confident in myself was when I went on a date with a new love interest. It was Halloween. We went to a bar and I dressed up in heels and a feminine outfit. My date wanted to know how I happened to own a pair of heels in my size—and how come I was walking so confidently in them. I brushed it off, with no grand explanation, claiming I was just good at it. For a night, I was in my element, fully able to be myself. I wanted more moments like this, but they were few and far between in the coming decades.

As life went on, I did what many in my position do: I presented as masculine. I eventually married a woman. We had two kids and raised a family. But for the better part of 25 years, I couldn't look at myself in the mirror. I would glance at my reflection and stare at the person looking back at me, and think, *Oh my god, you're not—that's not what I am.* The best way I can describe it is a scary, weird, and awkward feeling, to look at yourself and think, *Who the hell is this person looking back at me?* I didn't see myself like this. Logically, I understood it was my reflection—but internally that was not who I was or wanted to see looking back at me.

There were days when I would actually just sit in the shower and cry. It just hurt too much to look at that person. I just couldn't do it and there were a number of days when I would just get so overwhelmed that I couldn't hold any of it in anymore. I didn't identify with who I was looking at. There was one time that I actually punched through a mirror in my daughter's bedroom because I couldn't stand to see that reflection. It didn't matter if it was in a mirror or in pictures. Even as recently as a few years ago, when my daughter had her prom, I was brought back to this horror when I conceded to dressing up in a coat and tie, like a man, forced to pose for pictures. When they showed them to me, I broke down crying, my mind racing with thoughts like, *That's not me!* No one knew about the decades-long struggle I'd been having to come to terms with who I wanted to look like and how I wanted to present.

During this time, I began to see a therapist to work through the feelings I couldn't understand. During those early sessions which went on for ten years, I finally had a place to talk over the feelings I'd put down for so long. One of the first affirmations the therapist gave me was that I was not a cross-dresser.

They told me, "You do know you're trans, right?"

Part of me had known all of my life, way back to when I was playing with magic markers and dressing up in my mom's clothes, but hearing it out loud was a revelation. I thought back on everything that I had been through, everything that I had felt for so many years, and I thought to myself, *Yes, this is it!* Now everything could come together and my life could change.

Those were the words I needed to hear, but I still wanted multiple opinions and perspectives. It's a process to get approval for something you've denied your whole life. I sought out two more therapists and worked out more of what I'd been feeling. Each of them came to the same conclusion, and after getting confirmation from a third therapist, it gave me the confidence to assert that this was who I am—I wasn't making it up, nor was it something I had just woken up one day and decided to be. No, this had been a part of me for years—from the start of my life. Once I got here, the next question laid out in front of me was what I planned to do with this information. It was great to figure out who I was, but now I had to think about how I was going to express that, and how that was going to change my life and the lives of those around me, especially my family.

NAVIGATING FAMILY LIFE

Navigating the decision to be "me" took many years. I knew there would be consequences to transitioning—some were obvious, like the upheaval that would come to my life, through fallout with family or potentially losing my job, but I knew there would be plenty of other things that I could never

IT SUDDENLY HIT
ME THAT AFTER
NEARLY 50 YEARS
OF QUESTIONING,
**I WAS FINALLY
RECOGNIZED FOR
WHO I AM.** IT JUST
FELT PERFECT.

have predicted. My biggest fear was that I'd be left alone when all the dust settled. For that reason, I didn't immediately act on my desire to transition. Instead, I took time to consider all my decisions and how I could properly navigate my life in the long-term.

One pivotal moment came, seven years ago (from the time of this writing). My family was watching an NFL game and I wanted to step away and get dressed up, if only for a little bit. My teenage daughter entered my room, surprising me. I was in women's clothes.

"What's up?" she asked.

I was caught off guard. There was no excuse in the world that would be good enough to explain what she had just seen. So I told her the truth. I saw no point in hiding it.

I very honestly said, "I'm female and trans, and this is what it means."

She said, "Oh, okay," then turned around and went running down the stairs to tell my wife and my son. I went right behind her and explained what had happened and what I'd been feeling, and what I'd been keeping from them.

Up to this point, my wife had some idea about my cross-dressing, but not to the extent of wanting to transition and fully be myself. That Sunday, we planned to take things in stride, but ultimately, she never fully came around to accepting me for who I am. My son didn't want to know anything about it and outright rejected me. My daughter was the one who accepted me completely. Not long after, we all went to see a priest, who was also a family friend, to talk about my transition. It allowed me the opportunity to speak openly about what being trans meant for me. We continued to talk things through and had a good conversation together, or at least, I thought so. My wife and son were still not supportive.

I believe that because my teenage daughter had some friends who were gay, lesbian, or trans, she had the empathy to understand what I was going through and feeling. As a result, she became my biggest supporter—and fashion critic! I remember one time, right before she left to go to college, I came downstairs dressed to kill (or so I thought).

My daughter took one look at me and said, "Oh no, just no! Go back up and change."

In her own way, she has always looked out for me and made sure that I'm putting my best foot forward. Early on, she wrote me a really sweet note that I still have on my mirror upstairs. It says: "You 'girl' so much better than you ever 'guy-ed.'" Having that message from my daughter warms my heart every time I read it.

My daughter refers to me as 'Mom,' 'Dad,' and 'Caroline' interchangeably, depending on where we are and the social circumstances. For instance, if we're out in public, like at a grocery store, she'll refer to me as 'Mom.' It's a great feeling, being referred to in that way and hearing her say it, but at the same time, I'm fine with whatever she calls me. If she's at work, or with people she knows, she decides how she's going to refer to me, and whatever she chooses is fine. She's obviously not going to refer to me as 'Dad' when I'm out and presenting femininely, but I leave it up to her what she chooses to say and don't put any pressure on her. It's kind of cool, in a way—like, she had a few of her friends come over and hearing them refer to me as 'Ms.' meant a lot to me, and I didn't have to force it. She did it on her own and it was really nice to get that affirmation.

Despite the planning and decisions that went into my transition, my son never accepted me. Instead, like my wife, he actually made fun of me. Maybe it was just his way of coping. Throughout this journey, I've suffered the loss of many people close to me who were unwilling to accept me for me. It was part of the future I had predicted and knew was always a possibility—but despite so many in opposition, having even one person behind me, my daughter, makes all the difference. She remains my biggest supporter.

From the first moment I told my family I was trans, I presented only casually inside my home. At work, my position prevented me from coming out. After 20 years of working in financial services, which tends to be extremely conservative, I decided to leave and do something different, mainly so that I could fully present as myself. Occasionally, I would dress differently for business, but otherwise, I always presented as myself.

My wife's lack of support prevented me from moving forward with my transition. She said she didn't, "want to be married to a woman," nor did she want to have labels put on her by others. When I made my announcement about my gender identity, she decided to take her own actions and filed for a divorce. In the process, she outed me to my brothers, the neighbors, and anyone else she could. Maybe she needed people to confide in to help her through it, but it hurt because it was my story to tell, not hers. I spoke to her about it and she agreed to not tell my father or my employer, since it would put me at risk for discrimination and possible termination. I also asked her not to involve our friends at the church, but she did share with some, which resulted in my resigning from the church and activities, because it became very difficult.

PASSING THE TORCH

It's been about a year (as of this writing) since I officially changed my name and gender marker on my IDs. It was such an overwhelming and wonderful moment to go to the courthouse, and have a judge make it official. After reviewing the paperwork, the judge actually came down from the bench to give me a hug, telling me I was a great woman, and how happy they were for me to finally and fully be me. I could never have predicted that response and I was thrilled by it. Outside the courthouse, I sat in my car just looking over my gender change documentation and cried. I took several moments to take everything in and process what had just happened up to this point. I finally felt like me. This made it official. Nothing in the world can ever tell me that I'm not who I say I am and I can finally be me. It was time to head over to the Department of Motor Vehicles and get a new driver's license. Halfway there, all the emotions swelled up to the surface again and I had to pull over. It suddenly hit me that after nearly 50 years of questioning, I was finally recognized for who I am. It just felt perfect. I sobbed like a baby!

Waking up the next day was the most wonderful feeling in my life. I didn't have to think about anything. I didn't have to worry. I didn't have to think of myself as cross-dressing. I just got up and I was just me! It was the first time in my entire life that I felt like that. I didn't have a concern in the world that morning. It's funny, I was actually hoping that I'd get pulled over by the police that day, just so I could show them my license.

Later that day, I did get 'sir-ed' going through the checkout line in the grocery store. I just slapped down my driver's license and credit card, showing them that I was legally female. I didn't want to have a huge confrontation with the clerk, not that day. I simply showed the person that I was legally me and moved on.

If there was one thing I'd learned throughout my journey, it was to walk away from these situations. It's not worth it to try and engage with someone who may not listen—nor do I need to apologize for who I am. As trans people, we just need to live our lives and never care about what other people think of us.

That's when we take our power back and say, "You know what? I'm going to continue being me, and you'll continue being you, but you have no authority or influence over it."

That is something that I impart on other trans people, especially the younger trans people I meet when I travel and speak at my alma mater each year. When I attended, I had yet to transition, so to go there now and fully present as a female makes up for it. I make it a point to meet with a graduating trans person to offer my advice as they move into the working world. I impart my own experiences, while making assurances that, despite the difficulty, the time will come when everything comes together and it will all have been worth it. I also explain that the world of being trans isn't something to be concerned about at all. The world of being trans is actually better, because they've shown competence in a way that most people will never understand. The world of being trans is a world of being genuine in a way that most people never will. It's a way of standing up for yourself in a way that most people can't possibly appreciate.

It took me years to realize who I was after college, and I'm thrilled to think about helping people say, "Okay, you are who you are and let's do it. Let's rock this world."

It's refreshing to see more and more people being their authentic selves and embracing who they are. When I graduated, so many years ago, it was another time, one without the representation that I have seen in recent times. It's been amazing to see that representation grow throughout the years.

Every year, I'd find reasons to go back to my school—either to a football or basketball game, a conference—and I'd also go home to visit my dad. (It's ironic, I don't get homesick leaving my home, I get homesick leaving my alma mater.) Over the years, I've literally been there hundreds of times. I've spoken at conferences; I've been in career counseling sessions; I've been in hiring sessions; I've spoken on many different topics; I've even taught classes and lectured to a class at the law school. I give back as much as I can to the community and, in return, it's rewarding to watch the campus' trans community grow each and every year.

No matter where I am, I do what I can to help trans people. One time recently, I was having lunch with a very good friend whose daughter is trans. Before she came out, she'd asked me if I'd ever worn nail polish before. It was an awkward question to ask, but it suddenly struck me that it was the exact same thing that had been on my mind when I was around her age. When she did come out, I was there as a support to her and the family, and walked them through everything that they needed to know. It gives me life knowing that that young trans girl will be able to live the life that she wants to now and that she won't have to struggle as much or as long as I had to, stumbling through life, trying to figure everything out, and left without any answers. I'm able to pass the torch of authenticity onto the next generation. We're able to live our truths out together.

For her birthday about three years ago, I gave her a huge box of nail polish, as a nod to the question she asked me years ago and as a opportunity for her to showcase her authenticity.

I'M JUST ME

I identify myself as who I am. I don't think of myself as transgender. I don't think of myself as female or male or having altered myself in any way. I just wake up and I'm just me. It's not a "lifestyle." It's who I am. I certainly didn't wake up and think, *Okay, let me decide that I want to shave my legs and paint my nails every day for fun.* This is just who I am. There's never been a doubt about it in my mind and there never will be.

Throughout all of my life, this has been something that's at the core of who I am. Nothing led me down this path, other than coming to terms with who I am. It's been a tough road that I've navigated. But at the end of the day, it was worth it. I finally am who I am and it's just perfect. I love my life now; I would not change a single thing. There is nothing about this that I would change.

The biggest piece of advice that I can give to another trans or nonbinary person is to be brave. Stand up for yourself and take ownership of who you are. Don't worry about what other people think of you. I'm still trying to learn that myself but life is who you are; it's what you make of yourself—so own it! Life is short. We don't have much time to be with the people we want to be with. Be kind to those with whom you work and always be gentle. Be confident in who you are and just own it. Be who you are and don't care what other people think of you.

THE WORLD OF BEING
TRANS IS A WORLD
OF BEING GENUINE IN
A WAY THAT MOST
PEOPLE NEVER
WILL. **IT'S A WAY OF
STANDING UP FOR
YOURSELF IN A WAY
THAT MOST PEOPLE
CAN'T POSSIBLY
APPRECIATE.**

Even though I still maintain some anonymity, what I want people to know about my story is that I just waited too long. I waited until it was comfortable for me and I cost myself a lot of my precious life. I've worked with many students, coached and counseled people, and told them how to make it in this world. I lied to myself because, while I told them how to make it and be authentic, I wasn't living up to it myself.

It took a long time to finally step up to the plate and say, "Why aren't you doing this yourself?"

It's always easier to solve other people's problems than it is to solve your own. It's easier to worry about how your friend or family member is doing than it is to deal with problems that begin to pile onto each other. That isn't sustainable and it goes back to the idea that you can't help others until you help yourself, like putting your oxygen mask on in an airplane.' It boils down to looking in the mirror and figuring out who you are. For so many years, it's difficult to just look in the mirror—because you don't like what you're seeing in the reflection. You're scared and terrified of who you're looking at. It's like wearing a scratchy sweater; It itches and it's uncomfortable, and it doesn't look good when you see yourself in it. And you still wear it!

I'm saying, don't! Be honest and take the damn thing off!

The advice that I have to give to anyone reading is to look in the mirror and, if you're comfortable with who you are, then love it. If you're not, then do something about it. I can't tell you how many years I couldn't reconcile who I was and what I looked like but now, it's completely behind me. I'm free. I am who I see in the mirror and I hope that you will (or that you already do) feel the same way. If you don't, then take steps to be who you are.

It's never an easy decision or an easy path to walk. Trust me, in the end, it'll all be worth it.

Brooke Cooper

The Real Lives of Transgender and Nonbinary Humans

REX E. WILDE

Rex (they/them) is an LGBTQ+ speaker, educator, consultant, and founder of Rex Wilde Consulting. Through their work as a transgender inclusion trainer and consultant, educating workplaces to become transgender inclusive, they seek to make a deep impact for the transgender community. They share their journey of authenticity and how they came to understand themselves to inspire others to follow their own intuition and embrace their own truth.

CONFORMITY OR BUST

It wasn't until 2014, when I was 24 years old, that I came to understand myself as nonbinary. I was sitting in my car, parked on a neighborhood street next to a park. My best friend, who was my partner at the time, was sitting next to me in the passenger seat. They turned to me and asked, "Have you heard of the word 'nonbinary' before?" I had not and told them so. Hearing their explanation, a light bulb went off in my head. After having spent years floundering to understand myself, I was finally presented with a word that perfectly named my gender experience. *I am nonbinary*, I thought to myself, *Finally, this vital part of myself uncovered.*

I grew up in a rather traditional household. Both my parents come from conservative Christian upbringings. My mom is the pastor of a church and my dad has always held close to convention. I was born and raised in Huntington Beach, California (which is a rather conservative area itself) with my older brother Josh and younger sister Rachel. In my early years of life, we were in many ways considered the perfect all-American family. My brother played baseball and my dad coached the team. My sister, mom, and I were always cheering from the stands. We sat in the front row at church every Sunday, listening to my mom preach. Everyone around us saw an upstanding traditional Christian family.

I remember the first time I learned my dad's thoughts about LGBTQI+ people. We were in the car, listening to the radio, and the topic of gay marriage came up. He asked me what I thought about it.

I said, "If people love each other, who cares if they get married? Why does it matter?"

My dad smiled, "All I know is...It's Adam and Eve, not Adam and Steve."

I remember feeling uneasy, even a little bit sad. But I knew better than to argue with what he had said. Obedience was an understood value in our household. We continued the drive in silence.

Growing up in my household, there was not any room to live outside the expected norm. The idea that one of my siblings or I might be queer wasn't even a thought in my parents' head because, to them, it was an impossibility. The idea that one of us might be transgender, outrageous. The idea that one of us might be nonbinary...well, that word, let alone the concept, wasn't even in their vernacular.

So how was I, a nonbinary kid living in a household and society that only acknowledged heterosexuality and a two-gender system, supposed to know about gender identity?

Middle school was the first time I started to explore my gender presentation. Pop punk was all the rage, and heavy eyeliner and angular haircuts were the latest trend. Avril Lavigne started to become really big at that time. I remember seeing her in music videos on TV. Her appearance was simultaneously carefree and in your face. She was the first example I'd ever seen of androgyny. A woman wearing men's pants and acting as if she was "one of the boys." I was completely enamored. Looking at her, I was able to connect with a part of myself I hadn't seen before.

After school, I would often go with a group of my friends to the nearby thrift store, Savers. I was always drawn to the men's pants section and came home with a different pair each time. Always the colorful baggy men's Dickies pants that were so popular in the '90s and early 2000s. My favorite pair was teal—what I imagine a darker, more mysterious part of the ocean might look like. Wearing those pants was the first time I had ever experienced gender euphoria. I felt powerful, beautiful, and most importantly...I felt like myself.

It was not long into this newfound period of aesthetic exploration that my parents started to take notice. The more I wore baggy pants, studded belts, and dark eyeliner, the more concerned they became with my appearance. One night, they sat me down at the dinner table for us to have "a talk." They asked me where I had been getting my pants. They likely thought I was taking them from my brother. I told them I bought them from the thrift store. They were not pleased with this. They told me I wasn't to shop there anymore and that it was inappropriate for me to dress the way I had been.

At the time, I had no language to say that dressing this way was a part of my gender expression. That this was how I wanted to dress because it felt good and was authentic to me. My parents told me I was only allowed to go shopping with my mom from then on, and that I had to buy clothes that were "appropriate" for me. Me, who they saw as their oldest daughter. Me, who they worried would make a bad impression if their church friends saw how I was dressing. Me, who would now bear the brunt of their scrutiny and inability to recognize authenticity, even when it was right in front of them.

It wasn't just my parents who pressured me to maintain a traditional gender presentation. Once I started dressing more traditionally feminine, I noticed the reactions from all other people in my life. The more femininely I presented, the more compliments I got. People would tell me I was pretty and beautiful and would want to talk to me more because I looked how they expected me to. Of course, they didn't realize the impact this would have on me. To them, they were following what they had been taught. That because I was assigned female at birth, I must be a girl. And therefore, the only way for me to be in the world was as a Carrie Underwood or Celine Dion. Norm-abiding, traditional, feminine.

I was in middle school when I had my first crush on a girl. We had several classes together and I often caught myself staring at her, butterflies in my stomach, thinking of how wonderful it would be to hold her hand.

One of the kids in my homeroom somehow caught on that I had a crush on this girl and loudly made fun of me in front of her about it one day.

I responded defensively, "No! I do NOT have a crush on her!" But the weight of the truth haunted me—I wanted to tell her.

When I told my friends, they said, "You can't tell her. It's not going to end well."

One day after school, I decided to do it. My heart was beating in my throat. I found her in the courtyard and called out to her.

"Hey, Taylor!"

She walked over to me. I thought to myself, *It's now or never,* and with a glimmer of hope in my heart, I said, "Actually...I do have a crush on you."

She looked at me, wide-eyed, and then...she walked away without saying a word. I was left stunned, thinking, *Oh no. What did I do?* I felt everything shift in that moment. I knew I had made a huge mistake.

It only took the remainder of that afternoon for word to spread about what I had revealed to her. After that, I was made fun of constantly. Anytime I would stand near her or she was close by, someone would make a mocking comment about me. It was humiliating. And it embedded within me a clear message about how I was expected to be in the world. Not myself. Not honest. Not Queer.

These messages, from virtually everyone around me, left their mark. And it only compounded the traumatic experiences I had been through earlier in life.

At the age of seven and eight, I was continuously molested for a whole school year by my third grade teacher. The truth of this came out, and my parents, along with the parents of other children who had endured the same, sued the teacher. I remember going to court when I was in fifth grade, taking the stand to describe in detail what he did to me. Seven other students testified against him as well.

The verdict? Not guilty. This man, who had very clearly molested more than eight children, was found not guilty.

Later in life, my mom explained to me that the jury wanted to charge him as guilty, but that they were unable to charge him because of the language of the law.

Following the court case, my parents took me to see a psychologist. After seeing me for a couple of sessions, the psychologist told my parents that I wasn't ready to process this experience and advised my parents to continue to live and act as if everything was normal. So this deep trauma happened that my family didn't know how to deal with and the professional advice we received was to "just ignore it." That left me as a nine-year-old, trying to figure out how to deal with it on my own.

I left this experience with the internalization that, if the court found him not guilty, it must have meant I was lying or made it up. That it didn't really happen to me. I came to believe a horrific distortion—that people must not believe me when I tell the truth—because I told the truth that day in court and left thinking that nobody believed me. As I grew up, this led me to continuously second guess myself, my real experiences, and my truth.

Once I started high school, I felt increased pressure to hide the truth of my being queer. With the humiliation of middle school behind me, I had the opportunity to make a new reputation for myself. No one had to know I'd had a crush on a girl. And since I was attracted to people of multiple different genders, it was easy for me to put the past behind me and go along with "being straight." This is when I began to completely suppress my queerness. If I was going to be accepted, I needed to fit in. And in order to fit in, I needed to forget that I had ever worn men's clothes or had a crush on a girl.

REDISCOVERING TRUTH

I initially started college as a music major. I had been a singer throughout my life and began my studies in vocal perfor- mance, but I actually really struggled with it. Whenever I would get up to sing by myself in front of others, I would get intense stage fright. My body would shake and I could barely stand up straight. This is why I preferred singing in the choir. I was able to hide amongst the crowd, to sing without being singled out. Being alone in front of others is what caused me such intense anxiety.

It was frustrating because I deeply loved singing and I didn't understand why being onstage by myself was such a problem. What I realized later on, once I had come out as queer and nonbinary, was that I struggled because I was never taught to be confident in myself—my real self. Standing in front of others to sing alone, it made me feel naked and ashamed. Like I would be ridiculed just for existing, just as I had been in so many of my earlier life experiences.

While studying vocal performance my first year, I took a sociology class to fulfil my general education credits. For some reason, I felt really drawn to sociology and over the course of the class, I fell in love with the subject. I loved thinking about the ways that society shapes us as individ- uals and as a collective. I was fascinated by considering how our society was structured, and as someone who grew up with such a limited perspective of the world, I loved learning about new perspectives I'd never been exposed to. I grew up learning the "Golden Rule," to treat others how you want to be treated. And that if you work hard in life, you will prosper in your life and career. Sociology truly opened up avenues for me to see how narrow and mono- lithic those worldviews are. I understood that my perspective was limited, as someone who grew up in a white, affluent, Christian family that did not expose me to the wide variety of life experiences that exist.

From discovering this newfound love, and my continuous struggle with singing, I decided to change my major to sociology while keeping music as a minor. I believe this was a choice driven in part by my subconscious that was knocking at my heart, telling me to find my way back to myself and my truth.

Sociology offered me an entirely new way to learn about identity and therefore myself. One of the most influential classes I took was called "Social Stratification and Inequality." In this class, I started to learn for the first time about race, class, and how privilege and oppression play a vital role in how our society has historically functioned. This was something I never learned about growing up; my family never talked about class, and certainly never about race (aside from the ways in which racism was openly encouraged by my friends and family). There was never a discussion about privilege or about how my experience growing up white and affluent would be different from that of people of color or of a different socioeconomic status. This course drew a clear line throughout history that showed me the inequities people faced in the past and how they've led to the inequities that exist now. It completely blew my mind, and I was incredibly angry that nobody had ever taught me these things, that no one in my community had talked about them.

With a raging fire lit within me, I started to get involved in social justice, advocacy, and identity work. I started working with the LGBTQI+ community on campus. I joined a group that hosted "Safe Space" trainings to help folks learn about and become allies to the LGBTQI+ community. I eventually became a trainer, facilitating discussions and educating others about allyship, at the time seeing myself as a cis, straight woman.

At the end of my first year, I joined a sorority, Kappa Alpha Theta. I was a member of the inaugural class of a new chapter on my campus, something I was incredibly proud of. Through Kappa Alpha Theta, I met countless people that I absolutely adored, both in my sorority as well as in other Greek Life organizations on our campus. From chapter meetings to dance parties to charity events, I was completely immersed in Greek Life. I lived and breathed Greek Life, every minute of it.

As I became more aware of social inequities and the way they played out, not only in our larger society, but also directly on campus, I began to notice some ways in which the Greek Life system lacked awareness around social justice issues. One way was in seeing how Greek Life lacked any real education and understanding of LGBTQI+ people, which led me to work with other Greek Life leaders to create Safe Space trainings specifically tailored to sororities and fraternities.

Though the trainings were meant to provide education on the whole LGBTQI+ spectrum, the reality is that the trainings had more of a sexuality framework (how to be more inclusive of people who are lesbian, gay, or bisexual), with less emphasis on gender identity and the transgender community. As good as our intentions were as LGBTQI+ educators, there was a lack of understanding around gender diversity and trans people, even within the LGBTQI+ educational space. So those of us educators did the best we could in elevating the consciousness of the Greek community around LGBTQI+ allyship.

Me, all the while, still identifying as a cis straight woman.

During my junior year I went to a conference called Social Justice Training Institute for Students. It was a week-long educational conference where students from colleges across the country came together to deepen their knowledge around privilege and oppression. We were each split into different working groups, who we spent the majority of our time with, discussing our personal experiences around race, class, ability, sexuality, gender, etc. It was in one of these working group sessions where I first experienced a full discussion about how many of the LGBTQI+ members of the group personally identified as "queer." Though I had learned about it from a theoretical standpoint, I hadn't yet met anyone who specifically identified themselves as "queer." It was the first time I had gotten a personal explanation of what it meant.

I heard someone say: "To me, [being queer is] anything deviating from the norm of what's expected. It allows me the freedom of saying that I'm attracted to people of any gender..."

It was this conversation that led me to realize I might be queer. I remember being equal parts exhilarated and horrified. How was it possible that an idea made me feel seen but also scared the crap out of me? I knew that in order to figure this out, I had to tell someone. Later that night, I talked outside with a friend from my college, Morgan. I told her that I thought I might be queer, and I started sobbing.

She held me while I rocked back and forth and asked, "What's wrong with that? Why are you crying?"

"I don't know," I said.

After the conference, I started attending a confidential LGBTQI+ processing group on campus called Stonewall. It was there that I started to confront the reality of my shame. The horror I felt around my queerness came from all the messages I had internalized growing up, through my church, my family, even my school. Every community I had been a part of had told me that it wasn't okay to be queer. I was afraid that if the women in my sorority found out that they would see me as perverted or hate me. I feared that if my family found out, they would be disappointed. I worried that the many friends I had made throughout my college career would abandon me. These deep anxieties led me to become severely depressed.

I struggled a lot during my last two years of college. I was constantly having to navigate this new identity within my social circles. I had to figure out who was safe to tell and express this part of myself to, versus those who might react badly. I was able to be open within the social justice community but was terrified of telling almost everyone else. I had a deep desire to express this part of myself openly, but my past experiences convinced me that it was safest to keep it mostly under wraps.

My first job out of college was in political advocacy, continuing my goals of being an activist and educating the masses about LGBTQI+ people and identities. I worked for a third-party affiliate that partnered with the Human Rights Campaign to run fundraising initiatives through canvassing. I traveled throughout the country doing this work—finally living outside the Orange County bubble I had grown up in. It was my first time being in a brand-new group of people, who hadn't known me prior to my coming out, and who I knew would accept me fully. At long last, I felt comfortable fully expressing my queerness without hesitation. For once I could just be myself.

CRASH

Being able to express my queerness brought me an incred-ible freedom. I felt excited to date whoever I wanted, talk about myself openly, and not have to hide anything. At least, I didn't have to hide the things that I was aware of. But the reality was, I was still masking many other parts of myself. Uncovering my queerness was only one of many truths yet to be uncovered. The childhood traumas that I had yet to address, my gender identity—these were parts of myself that I was still running away from.

Throughout college and into my early career, I became a workaholic in order to cope, albeit unconsciously. During college, I was involved in every organization that I had interest in (ten of them), all while completing my major and minor, research and writing my senior thesis, becoming a Resident Advisor, and working a part time job. I spent every minute of every day doing something. There was a signifi-cant amount of time where I would only get two to four hours of sleep at night because I had so much to do. But that's how I coped with my trauma, with the internalized shame around my queerness, and the reality of my transness that I hadn't yet consciously realized.

With my organizing job, I often worked 80 hours a week. It was expected that we work at least six days a week, typically clocking a 12 to 14-hour work day. I would stay at the office until 10 p.m. and often functioned on four hours of sleep. I kept pushing myself—unknowingly running away from the pain of my past—but the truth was creeping up on me and I was growing increasingly anxious and depressed. I tried to ignore how I felt by pushing myself further, trying to avoid thinking about the root causes of my feelings.

The Real Lives of Transgender and Nonbinary Humans

I had been working my organizing job for about a year when I started having dangerous thoughts about wanting to hurt myself. It wasn't long until I knew that I needed help. I started seeing a therapist, who helped me realize that I wouldn't be able to take care of myself while continuing to work such a demanding job. I wanted to prioritize my health and decided to tell my supervisor what was going on with me.

I remember the conversation with my Regional Director. I asked if we could talk and he suggested we take a walk around the block while we chat. It was summer in Chicago. The day was bright, and there were folks walking along the streets, coming and going from wherever they were coming from and going to, a mid-level hum of mid-afternoon activity before the after-work rush.

"I hate to have this conversation...but I have to quit," I told him. "I'm not well. I have depression and it's been getting worse and worse. I can't do this job anymore because it takes too much time when I need to focus on myself. I have to give you my two weeks."

My boss looked at me sympathetically and said, "You know, this campaign really needs you. Can't you just stay a little longer? How about a month?"

It was completely manipulative and it worked. I felt guilty for even bringing this up in the first place. I had never learned how to take care of my mental health, let alone how to set boundaries. I ended up staying.

My commitment to staying another month did nothing to change my depression. The longer I stayed, the more depressed I became. The more depressed I became, the more frequent and more convincing my suicidal thoughts became.

One day, the heaviness of it all became too overwhelming. While working that day, I decided that that night I was going to go home and kill myself. As soon as I got home from work, I started drinking. I figured that this would take the edge off and give me enough courage to actually do it. While I started thinking about how I was going to act on this plan, I heard a voice in my head: *Call Susy.* Suzy was one of the best friends I had made in Chicago. I decided to listen to the voice, still playing a game with myself to bargain for suicide—to bargain for the only thing I thought would stop my pain.

I told myself that if she doesn't answer the phone, it's a sign that I should end my life, and if she does answer, then I live another day. I called and she picked up. I started sobbing, telling her what was going on. She told me not to do anything and that she was coming over immediately. When she got there, we went out onto my back porch so she could smoke a cigarette while we talked.

I asked her for a cigarette and she said, "This is the only circumstance where I'm going to say yes to you smoking a cigarette."

We smoked while we talked. I told her what I could about what was overwhelming me. She told me that I would not be staying at my apartment that night. She said that we would go to our friend Tina's house and would stay there together. Tina and Suzy had talked at some point and they knew I needed help.

I remember Tina's voice later that night, saying "We need to take you to the hospital. We don't have to do it right now, but we do have to tomorrow, so how about we get some food and just hang out together tonight?"

That's what we did. We spent the night together and the next day I was admitted to the psychiatric ward at Northwestern Hospital in downtown Chicago. I ended up being hospitalized for a week and then transferred into an outpatient program.

At the hospital, memories of all of the traumas that I had experienced rushed back to me: being assaulted as a kid, growing up in a toxic household, and thinking that being honest and authentic was wrong and not believable. I thought that people didn't want me to be the way that I was, that who I was at the core was wrong.

I had been hiding from these truths for so long, had buried them deep, deep down, so as to never have to experience their undeniable pain. But this was their uncovering. It was like an archeological dig that would take years of discovery and unearthing to fully uncover everything that had been buried over the years. The soil had been loosened and I could feel them each trying to lift themselves up to be seen. It was now my turn to figure out how to uncover them fully, how to dig through to find myself, and how to dig myself out.

RECOVERING AND UNCOVERING

After being discharged from the hospital, I was enrolled in an intensive outpatient program (IOP). Understanding that I would need to fully commit myself to mental health recovery for the foreseeable future, I decided to move back to California to live with my mom. The IOP I joined in California required that I attend therapeutic sessions, both group and individual, for six hours a day, five days a week. It was like going to school for your mental health. Instead of studying theories and concepts, you had to study yourself.

In this program, I was encouraged to explore the realities of past traumas I'd experienced. Not only to recognize their reality, but to understand the ways in which my psyche was still responding as if those traumas were present day threats. This was meant to provide me with an access point to better understand and take care of myself. It was deeply uncomfortable and often frightening. There were many times where I had panic attacks for multiple days in a row. I had to learn how to soothe myself through these, while also allowing myself to experience the very real emotions that came up, rather than suppressing them like I had been taught to my whole life prior.

By finally allowing myself to explore my past experiences and the emotions that accompanied them, as well as having a team of professionals and a community of others working through their own mental health recovery, I was able to continue to uncover parts of myself that I had long since buried.

When I left Chicago, a good friend of mine gave me one of his flannel shirts as a memento. It wasn't something I ever thought to wear, at least initially, but I kept it hung up in my closet with the rest of my clothes. One day, while I was playing around with my hair and makeup, I decided to try the shirt on—I thought out of boredom, though likely out of subconscious curiosity. It was the first time I had put on a piece of men's clothing since I was a kid. I looked in the mirror and my reaction was a swell of different emotions all at once. I felt completely repulsed, and simultaneously curious and fascinated. I was equal parts terrified of and enamored with myself. I hated looking at myself. But I also had a nagging growing louder in my mind—*Why? Why do I hate this so much?* I had to take a step back and unpack everything that I was feeling. These mixed emotions revealed deeply rooted internalized shame around wearing men's clothes and having a gender expression that deviated from traditional social norms. It was the first time I felt a calling to explore these feelings deeper.

In the years following this experience, I became much more fluid in how I expressed my gender. I started buying men's clothes and felt confident when wearing them. The more I explored myself through my wardrobe and aesthetics, the more it felt like there was something else that was bubbling beneath the surface.

Then came that fateful day, sitting in the car by the park, when I heard the word 'nonbinary' for the first time. *I am nonbinary*, I thought to myself. More soil had been lifted. Finally, another vital part of myself uncovered.

OPENING UP

Learning about the concept of nonbinary was an awakening for me. A few months after this new element of self-discovery, I started to come out to people. First, to my roommates and close friends. Shortly after coming out to them I changed my name to Rex, a name I felt was perfectly suited for me in my androgyny and nonbinary identity. Eventually, I came out more publicly to my community of friends on Facebook, and slowly, over the course of a couple of years, to my family. There was no way for me to predict how my parents and family would react to coming out as nonbinary. Considering that the concept would be entirely new to them, I expected (and prepared for) some level of rejection.

When I came out to my mom, her first words were, "Honey, I love you so much. I can't imagine how hard this must be for you."

MY JOURNEY HAS
BEEN FULL AND IT'S
BEEN BEAUTIFUL,
SAD, EXCITING,
UNCERTAIN, CLEAR,
AND ABOVE ALL,
**IT'S BEEN REALLY
FUCKING HUMAN.**

Her empathy meant so much to me. And while her response was loving and empathetic, there was still much for her to learn before she was able to be truly affirming of me.

My mom initially struggled with connecting her intentions of love with her actions in supporting me and my identity. She had a hard time understanding they/them pronouns because of the way she learned pronouns in school. She told me she had it "drilled into her" to never use they/them for a single person, and it was something she had to unpack and unlearn. She also had a lot of fear around what it would be like for me in the world, especially once I went on testosterone.

"Wouldn't it just be easier if you were a man?" she said to me one day.

Being a nonbinary and visibly trans person is in no way easy in a world that has rigid expectations around gender and most often does not recognize people of third genders. I am sure that it would be easier, in some respects, if I were a binary man, but it certainly wouldn't be me.

As my mom struggled to understand my identity and how to be supportive of me, our relationship became very strained. Though I knew she loved me unquestionably, it was difficult trying to help her understand my identity and the ways I was changing to express my truth. My sister became an integral part of my mom learning what she needed to in order to fully respect me. Rachel sat with our mom through many con- versations, patiently explaining to her things about gender and transness that I did not have the emotional capacity for.

My sister had a deeper understanding of trans people, and nonbinary folks especially, because one of her best friends since high school, Brett, was trans. Brett was actually the very first trans person I ever (knowingly) met. When I came out as nonbinary, Brett and I had many conversations about being trans and nonbinary. Once I told them I use they/them pronouns, it helped them realize that they were also nonbinary and wanted to use they/them pronouns as well. That brought us closer together. I felt lucky to have someone so close to my life and my family who I could share this part of myself with and be understood by.

As I continued to navigate my relationship with my family, myself, and what it was like to be a trans person in this world, I also explored different avenues in my career path. For several years, I worked a public speaking job for a medical company, which led me to realize the talent I had for public speaking. I knew I wanted to somehow use this skill to uplift transgender and nonbinary people's voices and help the community in a more direct way. In 2017, about four years after I came out as nonbinary, I started working for an organization called Trans Can Work, where I was able to put my experience in advocacy and public speaking to work. This organization aimed to connect trans individuals to jobs with inclusive employers. It was a brand-new organization and I was their first employee. I was tasked with building a jobs program to serve the trans and gender expansive community in California, while also training employers on transgender inclusion in the workplace. I was absolutely thrilled to be able to serve my community in this way.

Just about a month into starting this new position, my sister and I moved together to Pasadena. At that time, we had been spending a lot of time with Brett and knew they were struggling with their mental health. Brett had schizophrenia. There would be times when they would be fully present with my sister and me, and then suddenly, it was like they weren't there. Physically, they were there, but emotionally and mentally, it felt like they disappeared. It was a strange energetic shift. My sister and I found out later they would hear voices and they would see people who weren't really there but saying horrible things to them. The voices would tell them they were worthless, that they shouldn't live.

When Rachel and I moved, Brett often stayed with us. They would stay at our house for days at a time but when they left to go back to their parents' house, their mental health got worse. There were many things plaguing them, including stress about how to live in the world as a trans person. On the evening of Valentine's Day of 2017, I got a text from my sister, "Brett is gone." We lost them to suicide that day.

That night, I cried and screamed and wailed, alone in my living room. Begging the Universe for this not to be true. For it to take anyone else, just not my Brett.

The pain of losing Brett in this torturously traumatic way was monstrous. It felt as though my heart had been shattered into a million pieces. Why did they have to be taken away?

Brett was an incredible person. They had a deep sense of spirituality and interconnectedness. They believed in such goodness and purity; the great potential this world has for goodness and the inherent purity within us all. One of the last things we did together was go to the Women's March, just two weeks before their death. They posted on Facebook that night about the power we create when we come together collectively to stand up for unity and justice. They had a deep passion, not only for political advocacy but also for collective healing. They believed that when we heal ourselves as individuals, we heal the world.

Their belief in the world and in spirituality affected me deeply, especially after their passing. After they died, I made a promise to them to take care of myself and my mental health; to elevate my life in the ways that I know they desired to elevate theirs; and to impact this world in a way that would make it a better place for them to live in their next life.

I think about Brett every day. They will always live with me, in all that I am and in all that I do. Most days, I wear an old pendant of theirs, reminding myself they are with me wherever I go.

FINDING MY PLACE

After Brett died, I had to take some time away from work to grieve and reassess my life's priorities. I took time to study music at a local community college and even considered a career in music therapy, always with my eyes on how I could serve the trans and gender expansive community.

When I was ready to return to work, I started picking up different projects. One of them was with an organization called My LGBTQ+ School. The organization focused specifically on educating individuals who had no prior exposure to the LGBTQI+ community. I developed educational campaigns and creative content, focusing on how to effectively educate people who were brand-new to topics of LGBTQI+ inclusion. It was one of several experiences that reinvigorated my passion for education and activism, what I had started in college and continued in the other educational work in the LGBTQI+ community that I had been doing for years.

I eventually went back to work with Trans Can Work, this time as their Program Director and lead trainer. I continued building off of my previous work, creating a jobs program for the TGNC community while also conducting transgender inclusion trainings for businesses. Our goal was to get 60 individuals hired by inclusive employers within the first year.

In order to meet this goal, I collaborated with a close friend of mine, Jason Hill, to organize a transgender career fair called Transcend. We worked together for six months to put on the Transcend Career Fair, with over 75 businesses and 500 transgender job seekers participating. It was incredible seeing the number of people who showed up and getting to collaborate with so many businesses and community organizations. It ended up being the largest transgender career fair in the world. By the end of the year, we saw over 100 individuals hired into new positions.

Throughout this year, I also flew all over the country to provide transgender inclusion trainings for businesses, helping to cultivate more inclusive employers. I provided 65 training sessions and trained over 200 participating businesses. As much as I loved working directly in the community, I knew my voice and talents were best used to engage people through the trainings I offered. That was where I was meant to be, where my work has the greatest impact.

After seeing the turnout at the Transcend Career Fair, it became clear to me how much work there was to be done in creating workplaces where TGNC people felt they could bring their full selves to work. For years leading up to this, my intuition had been nudging me to use my experience as an educator to dedicate myself fully to working with employers to create inclusive workplaces.

In June 2019, I left Trans Can Work to focus full-time on consulting and gender inclusion training, and started my business Rex Wilde Consulting. My mission has always been and will always be to create more inclusive environments for transgender, nonbinary, and gender non-conforming people to live fully and authentically. I believe the best way to do that is through educating cisgender individuals. With the unemployment rate of transgender individuals being three times the national average, workplaces are one of the best ways we can educate the masses and create more inclusive environments for TGNC individuals and communities.

This work means so much to me, because I know firsthand how life changing it can be for a trans person to feel seen and secure, both in the world and at work. I know that for someone like Brett, who struggled with job security throughout their life, in part due to their gender experience, that having people truly see them could have saved their life.

From being an LGBTQI+ educator in college, to talking with everyday people about LGBTQI+ issues in their homes and on the streets through canvassing, to working directly in the community to provide employment services to the TGNC community, I have learned a lot about how to effectively educate others. I've found that building empathy is one of the greatest ways to bridge understanding between the TGNC community and the rest of the world. And to do that, we have to start with how we connect with each other at a human level. I understand that most people have not met a transgender person and have had very limited exposure to transgender experiences. Because of that, it is important to approach education by meeting people where they are and walking forward together, not shaming them for what they do not know.

After finishing a training, I usually talk to participants one-on-one to answer additional questions or hear how the training landed for them. There have been countless people who have shared with me that the training was particularly helpful to them because they have a child (or a cousin, or brother-in-law, or friend) who is trans, and now they have more insight to better understand and support them. They also leave the training with tools to educate others in their circles, which I know continues to have a ripple effect as more people come out as trans or nonbinary every day. I often think about what the world will look like 5, 10, 20 years from now. It is only going to become even more gender diverse than it already is—I think more so than most of us can even imagine. And that, to me, is incredibly exciting.

BEAUTY IN COMPLEXITY

We are each on our own path. Wherever we are, we're all moving towards authenticity, and understanding what that looks like for ourselves. My journey has been full and it's been beautiful, sad, exciting, uncertain, clear, and above all, it's been really fucking human. I'm much more intentional now with how I build my life than I ever have been before, and that has helped me make the most meaning out of life. I'm no longer afraid of the complexity of life and when I feel fear, I sit with it rather than pushing it away. I've discovered how to sit in the complexity of life with a level of acceptance that I didn't have before.

My story is still being written and there will be more ups and downs as I continue on. What I've learned is that it's important for me to build an authentic relationship with myself, where I both nurture myself and challenge myself to better this world in the ways that I'd like to see it evolve.

For any trans or nonbinary person reading this, my advice to you is to find your people, whether that's other trans and nonbinary people, or any people who really love you, accept you, and are excited to have you in their life. Find people who you can be yourself around because you deserve to be you and to express yourself fully and completely. You deserve to experience all the complexity of being human, just like anyone else. It can feel isolating when we don't have space to do that, so find your people and trust that they're there to love you, show up for you, and be with you in whatever way you need them to be.

I want you to know that with all of the difficulties each of us experiences in life, healing is possible. Healing is a journey. I certainly haven't figured everything out, but I at least show up on the path every day. It's in the showing up that life happens and it's in the showing up that I found ways to make meaning out of my own life. I have found love for myself in the complexity of my life and I know that that can be true for anyone. It is by no means easy, but it is and always will be absolutely worth it.

Rex E. Wilde

BRANDI LAI

Brandi Lai (she/her) is the founder and president of Best Laid Pens, a ghostwriting and content strategy business that helps diverse people tell their stories. She has had the pleasure and privilege of bringing the stories in this book to life. Her mission is to give voices in her community a microphone so their truths can be heard. She hopes to continue to uplift the people around her and help them share their stories.

A EUPHORIC DISCOVERY

The idea of gender didn't cross my mind until I was about five or six years old. I was raised Catholic and I prayed some nights before I went to sleep. One night, I asked God if he could make me a girl but only for a short time. Something inside me wanted to know what that experience was like and how I would feel. I thought about it for a few nights after that, but the thoughts soon left me and didn't resurface for years.

In school, I tended to spend more time with girls than boys. I got along better with them and enjoyed being around them more. I didn't know why, but it wasn't something I was concerned about. I didn't question it, but internally I felt I was different from the other boys in my class. At the time, I thought it was because I was shy and introverted.

It wasn't until the summer between sixth and seventh grade that things started to click. I was sitting with my mom and sister Emily in the living room and they were watching an episode of *Friends*. One of the characters started talking about how much better the girls' clothes were, and that got my attention. I was curious: *Was he right, are they better?* I had to find out.

The next morning I woke up early. Emily and I were the only ones in the house. While she was still sleeping, I went into my parents' room and started to try my mom's things on. Turned out, the character was right: everything that I tried on felt so much better than my boy clothes. I felt that these clothes were what I should be wearing, and it wasn't until later that I realized what I was feeling, being happy with what I was wearing and what I was seeing in the mirror, was gender euphoria.

I put away everything I had tried on and kept this new discovery to myself. But I continued playing around at home with girls' clothes until the middle of seventh grade. At that point, I didn't see any deeper meaning in what I was doing. The thoughts and desires to try on girls' clothes left me until a few years later.

Growing up and going shopping for clothes, nothing ever felt quite right. I never had style. I remember my mom saying that I should care more about what I wore, but I could never find anything I liked. I didn't like the styles that the other boys in my class were wearing, but I could never find anything different that I liked and that stuck with me. I stayed within what was socially acceptable for boys to wear but always felt I was weird because my clothes felt wrong compared to what the other boys were wearing.

When I was a freshman in high school, Emily was a senior. We didn't get to spend a lot of time together, but one thing she wanted to do with me was to dress up for Spirit Week. Each day had a different theme and everyone dressed up based on that theme. There was Superhero Day and Nerd Day, and Emily and I dressed up for Wacky Tacky Day, wearing a mishmash of random clothes all thrown together. It was fun, and I knew I wanted to do it again the following year.

When I was a sophomore, as Spirit Week approached, my friend Kylie brought up the idea of painting my nails and doing my makeup. I was super excited, and we did a practice round the day before, where she painted my nails all different colors and put on my makeup. My parents were put off, but I thought it was harmless play. For me at the time, it was just a fun experience.

The next morning, Kylie did my makeup before school, and I turned more than a few heads as I went into class. Most people didn't read too much into it, at least from what I could tell, and just went along with it because it was Spirit Week and I was the weird kid.

When I got home from school that day, I was saddened, knowing I would have to remove the makeup and nail polish. At the time, I thought the feeling was just about a fun day ending, but below the surface, I knew there was something else. Something just felt right about the makeup and nail polish. I didn't have the words to describe what I felt, but I did take multiple pictures to commemorate the day.

I dressed up for Spirit Week again my junior year and I had a similar experience. It wasn't until that January that something inside spoke to me. I was in the bathroom that I had shared with my sister growing up. Even though she had already moved out of my parents' house, she had left behind a lot of her makeup in the bathroom, and I was curious about it. I had messed around with makeup for Spirit Week the past two years, so it wasn't totally foreign. I reached out and grabbed a tube of eyeliner. It was like I was operating on instinct, like it was calling out to me, and I held it in front of me, looking in the mirror. I stared at the tube and then a voice inside me spoke, *You've been able to go back and forth for so long, but if you put on that eyeliner, there is no going back this time.*

I knew exactly what that meant even if I didn't know where it would lead me. I knew that if I put on that eyeliner, it would be simply because I wanted to. There was no Spirit Week, no special event, no other reason other than it felt right, and I would have to figure out what it meant. I hesitated, but I knew the right thing to do was to follow my heart.

FINDING MY LANGUAGE

I put on the eyeliner and sat with myself for a moment, look-ing at myself in the mirror. It wasn't perfect but I was happy. After a few minutes in the bathroom, I took it off and I turned to the internet to try to figure out what I was feeling. I found a lot of YouTube videos talking about cross-dressing and it was like a 101 for newcomers. 'Cross-dresser' was the first term that I had, so I figured that's what I was.

I watched more and more videos, and there was one in particular that made me stop and question.

The person I was watching said, "Before you get too deep into this, you have to decide whether or not, for a lack of a better term, this is a hobby or if this is who you are. You have to decide that for yourself."

At first, I thought, *Of course this is just a hobby. I was able to stop before, when I was a kid, and I don't think there's any other deeper desire…right?* For a few days, I couldn't get the question out of my head. The more I thought about it, the more I started wondering, *What if this is something more, what if this is who I am?*

I decided to do more research and digging, and that's when I learned the word 'transgender.' Everything I read fit me to a T, and I started to connect past feelings and actions to what I now know as gender dysphoria and euphoria. I searched through forums and resources online, wanting to learn everything I could about what it means to be trans. I learned about Hormone Replacement Therapy, the struggle of coming out to other people, how to legally transition, and a lot of other information. The more I learned and explored, the more it felt like the pieces of my gender were coming together. I finally understood that I was trans.

COMING OUT BEGINS

It was great that I had all this knowledge about myself and about the trans community, but I had no one in my life I could talk to about this, which was isolating. I was too shy and introverted to reach out to people online, so I kept everything to myself until the summer between junior and senior year.

One day in early July, I went with two of my friends to the mall and surrounding areas. Some part of me knew I should come out to them. I needed someone to confide in and talk to about what was happening and what I was feeling. So I came out to them and they took it well. One of my friends, Vanna, who I'm still good friends with to this day, was ecstatic because she was the youngest of her sisters, and now she had someone she could mentor about clothes, fashion, and makeup.

Vanna taught me so much about being a girl. Soon after I came out to her, we started going to thrift stores, and she helped me pick out clothes. For a short while, she held onto the clothes we bought at her place; she would also let me pick and choose from clothes she was getting rid of, and she gave me makeup she wasn't using. She helped get my start, and I'll always be grateful for everything she's done for me.

Soon after that, I came out to a couple of other close friends, and I was met with overwhelming support. I couldn't be myself in school, but I was so happy to have supportive friends. At the time, it was fall of senior year, close to Spirit Week and Halloween. I wasn't sure how my parents were going to react to me coming out to them, so I thought I would try and gauge what their reactions might be. I decided to dress up as my authentic self for Halloween and write it off as a Halloween costume for the people I hadn't come out to yet.

I started preparing. Vanna had given me two dresses to choose from, and she and I went and got a pair of shoes that would match. The next thing I needed was a wig, as my hair was always cut short. The first time I put on that wig, I had just gotten out of the Halloween store. I looked in the mirror of my car and started crying. I was so happy to see who was finally looking back at me. I felt like myself for the first time in my life. I felt like I could finally point to my reflection and say, "That's me."

I went out that night with some friends and I felt free, like I could finally just be myself. I made sure to take in everything I was feeling. I took a ton of pictures and posted them on Facebook, and my dad commented on the picture, saying, "I didn't know I had a second daughter." Little did he know how right he was.

My parents didn't seem to have any reaction after they saw the pictures, at least from what I could tell. After Halloween, I wanted to dress up again for Spirit Week. I wanted to be myself again in public, even if it was only one more day. My mom and dad were a little apprehensive about the idea and questioned why I was doing it. I told them that it was just a fun thing to do for Spirit Week, and I ended up dressing up as myself for character day. I got a ton of questions about what I was and who I was dressed up as, and I came up with different answers each time.

I thought everything went well, but I still didn't have any idea how my parents would react if they knew the whole truth. About a month later, I still had the clothes that Vanna had given me in my closet, and I remember my mom was in there, talking to me about the SATs in my room. She happened to notice the clothes, and she asked why I still had them. I told her that I just hadn't given them back yet.

She said sharply, "Well you need to get rid of them."

Her tone, paired with her initial reactions to Halloween and Spirit Week, made me think she would not take things well.

I started to worry more and more about what might happen when I came out to my family, and by January of my senior year, I knew that I needed to talk to Emily about what I was feeling and get her perspective. She came home one night and we all went out as a family to a restaurant. She and I rode in her car, while my parents went in the other. It seemed to be as good a time as any to finally come out to her, though I waited until we were about to pull into the restaurant to say it because I was so anxious about what her reaction would be.

When I told her, her first response was, "I figured."

Now I was the one who was surprised! She told me that she picked up on me being trans because my profile picture on Facebook was from Spirit Week, where I posed with another friend of mine, and I was dressed in Vanna's clothes. We had a little bit of time to talk about things before we had to rejoin our parents. She was, and is, extremely supportive of me. When we talked about how our parents would react to me coming out, she also wasn't sure how things would go.

WAITING

My coming out process continued. My psychology teacher mentioned one day how she had a trans student in the past who wanted to be with the girls when they split up the boys and girls, and she told us her response was that they could choose whichever side they liked. I'm not sure why she brought it up, but in my head, I thought it was an opening, that I could potentially come out to her and she would be supportive.

After class, I waited for everyone to leave before telling her that I was trans. She asked me if I wanted to talk to the school guidance counselor about what I was going through and what I was feeling, and I said yes. I thought that by talking to the counselor, I could get some advice and insight on what I should do and how.

I went to the appointment that she made for me and I sat down and talked to the counselor about what was happening and what I was feeling. She asked me questions about my parents' background, trying to gauge how they would react. She asked about my parents' races and I told her my dad is Chinese and my mom is Colombian. She thought they might have some traditional thinking about LGBTQ+ people and they might react poorly because of it. That lined up with what my fears were. I had similar concerns and was already worried that they were going to kick me out or disown me. Her advice was to wait to tell them until after graduation (six months away)or until I was in college, so they could have time to process on their own.

I took her advice to heart and I initially thought this was the best way for me. But when I thought about how long it would be before I could come out and start to be myself, I got more and more depressed thinking about it. I started having suicidal thoughts, thinking only of the worst-case scenario that could happen when I came out. One night, I went to the bathroom and I just stared at myself in the mirror. I went and got my wig, put it on, and stared deeper, thinking that I could never be the person I was looking at. I started crying and curled up into a ball on the floor, feeling hopeless about the possibility of anything ever changing.

I kept myself going, just trying to get through each day. In class, I would think about and research the therapists I would see to get on HRT. I tried to focus on school, and I told myself that this wasn't going to last forever. I started to wish I had told my parents how I felt back in sixth grade, so I could have seen a therapist and been on the track for puberty blockers or HRT. I counted down the days to graduation and college.

It was a grueling couple of months, but things happened faster than I expected. I asked Emily if I could use her closet to store the clothes I had accumulated, since she wasn't living in our parents' house. She agreed, and I put all the clothes I had bought or that had been handed down to me in there. I thought everything was fine until one day, when my mom went in and noticed the new clothing in Emily's closet. She didn't say anything but I knew she knew what had happened.

They waited until Emily came home to have a family meeting to talk to me about what they had found; ironically, I had asked Emily if this was the right time to come out to them. They brought up the clothes and I explained everything.

Once I finished, the first thing that my dad had said was, "I wish you would have told us back in sixth grade, so we could have gotten you the therapy you wanted. We will always love you."

We all started crying and my mom said the same thing to me: "We will always love you."

SOME SUPPORT, SOME DISCOURAGEMENT

I felt overwhelmed with relief to have their support, and I wrote out everything I knew about being trans so that they had a baseline to start from. They helped me get into therapy when I started college at USF, which helped me tremendously. I was nervous about going on hormones, but I was finally able to talk to someone about it, even though I wasn't able to start my transition yet. I was ready to move quickly because I had already had time to think about it and decide about hormones, but my parents had just been introduced to this idea. They met with my therapist and we talked about my new name and the changes I wanted to make.

My mom's response was, "I don't think I can ever call you Brandi."

It hurt hearing that, and a few weeks later my dad talked to me and said, "You're freaking your mom out with what you're talking about."

For me, this meant I couldn't move forward. I couldn't go on hormones and I shouldn't talk about it.

I was discouraged and disheartened and I thought I had to keep everything to myself, but I didn't want to stop being myself. So during my second semester of college, I stepped out into class as myself. I emailed all my teachers and told them my new name and pronouns but I kept my head down. I didn't want to draw attention to myself, worried what people might think or say about me. It was a great feeling, being able to be myself in college, but I knew that when I went home to my parents, I had to be someone else.

This continued throughout 2015, my second and third semester of college, until I couldn't take it anymore. I couldn't stand not being able to fully be present as my true self. I started doing some research into any way that I could increase my estrogen levels without fully committing to HRT, and I scheduled an appointment with an on-campus doctor to talk about my options. He told me that I should consider taking a small dosage of HRT, which would delay the full effects from taking place and give me time to figure everything out. I thought this was what I needed, so I got the letter from my therapist and I started taking hormones.

FOR THE FIRST TIME IN
MY LIFE, I FELT LIKE
I WAS FULLY MYSELF.
**I FINALLY HAD THE
CONFIDENCE IN MYSELF
TO DO EVERYTHING
I HAD BEEN AFRAID
OF DOING** BECAUSE OF
MY BODY, AND I WAS
GOING TO TAKE EVERY
OPPORTUNITY TO MAKE
SURE I ENJOYED IT.

MY CHOICE, MY JOURNEY

I started HRT in 2016 because I was ready for things to change. I didn't want to continue living this double life, where I'm one person in college and someone else at home. Starting HRT gave me a time frame for when the physical effects would start to happen, when people would start noticing changes in me and perhaps ask me questions. I wanted to be prepared.

So I started coming out to close family members and friends: my best friend from high school, my cousin, my tía, and my tío. They all supported and accepted me for myself, and I was happy I was making some progress.

The next thing that I needed to do was to talk to my parents again about my transition. I brought it up with my dad and he agreed that it was something we should have been talking about more in the past year. All we could do was try and make up for lost time. We talked about it on and off during the months that followed.

The last thing I needed to do was to let my parents know that I was on HRT. I took them to a PFLAG meeting (Parents, Families and Friends of Lesbians and Gays) and a local support group meeting for parents of trans kids. They got to hear from other parents and learn from their experiences. They could relate to the other parents and learn more about what it means to be trans.

The morning before one of the meetings, my dad texted me asking to meet up and said, "How about you go as yourself and we'll go as your parents?"

I was over the moon, so happy I could finally be myself around my parents. I was nervous leading up to the moment that they saw me as me. That first moment we saw each other we said hello and gave each other a hug. We were with a group of people, so we didn't have time to talk too much with ourselves and things felt normal in the moments after. They saw that I was still me and that the only thing that was going to change was my outside appearance. We talked further when we went out to dinner that night, and we all started to get more relaxed and comfortable as the night went on. I was finally able to tell them what was happening, which enabled me to start on a higher dosage of HRT.

Everything seemed like it was going well and the promise I had made to myself that year was being fulfilled. Thanksgiving was approaching, a time when my parents, sister, tíos, cousin, and my tíos' parents usually come together to celebrate. The problem was that I had not come out to my tíos' parents yet, and my parents and I weren't sure how they would take it. We decided that I would pretend as if nothing had changed with me and wait until after the holidays to come out.

Originally, I thought I could do it, that I would be able to manage pretending, but the day of Thanksgiving, when I heard my voice drop again after fighting so hard to be me, I felt mortified. I felt so depressed and was counting down the seconds that I would have to wear this mask and pretend like everything was okay. I talked with my dad about how I felt the day after Thanksgiving and he came out to my tíos' parents for me. I never knew what their reaction was, but they seemed to accept it. I was just glad I didn't have to wear that mask again for Christmas and that I could finally have a Christmas where I could be myself.

A New Direction: School and Activism

My academic life began to change as I came out and as my transition progressed. I started out as a computer engineering major and quickly moved into computer science, but in 2016 I started to take classes in Women and Gender Studies (WGS). Every class that I took left me wanting to learn more. Those courses, along with encouragement from newfound friends from the class, helped me realize that I am a writer. I had written back in high school but never anything outside of stories that I would write for class; until that moment, I had never thought about writing as something I would pursue professionally.

WGS teachers assigned us essays or papers instead of projects or tests, and we'd often review each other's papers for feedback and advice. A lot of my friends encouraged me and told me that my writing was great. Because of that encouragement, I asked my friend Katie, who was an editor for *Her Campus* (an online blog for universities and colleges), if I could write for them. She said yes, and I started writing posts about different aspects of being trans along with current events. It was a great start and I was happy I was able to share my writing with other people, hoping it would impact people's lives. That was the start I needed to feel more confident in my writing, and towards the end of my degree, I was able to share my research paper with the South East Women's Studies Association (SEWSA). My research was about gender policing that I had seen within the trans community and the reasons behind that. It was an incredibly validating experience and showed that I can give a voice to issues and people through my writing.

Following Trump's election in 2016, my friends and I wanted to be more politically active than ever. We wanted to see and create change both at our college and in the surrounding community. We got more involved with local organizations and we all took a class that looked deeper into social movements, which helped us start our own efforts. As a class, we had to think about different issues affecting the campus and how we could organize around those issues. We each came up with different ideas, but ultimately, we decided to focus on campus dorms to make sure that they were equal, equitable, and inclusive for all students. Soon after, we broadened that mission to the college as a whole; since college was home for a lot of people, Safe HOME was born, with HOME standing for Housing Opportunities Made Equal.

We hosted multiple events, drawing attention to the inequalities we noticed on campus, and worked with the administration to make sure they were making changes and addressing those inequalities. Doing that work was inspiring and it made me realize the power that people have when we come together to create change. It takes tons of people to make sure that meaningful change happens, and it takes the support of a community to keep those people going. I'm proud of the work we did, and from those experiences, I was able to educate people in the community about what it means to be trans and how to be inclusive of the trans community. We created USF's first Slut Walk, an event giving survivors of sexual assault and sexual violence the chance to speak about their experiences as well as drawing attention to USF's own policies and practices when a student has been a victim. We worked with Planned Parenthood and rallied with them at multiple events in the area. We worked to educate the student body on issues like gender and sexuality, and later, shared our knowledge with students who were looking to create their own organizations for change. Through it all, I was able to work with diverse leaders and I knew that after graduation, I wanted to continue to educate people and create a more inclusive world.

While this was happening, I was getting ready for gender confirmation surgery (GCS). I knew that if I wanted to move forward with my life, I needed GCS. I was fortunate that my parents both supported me and that they were able to help me get surgery. I was incredibly nervous leading up to it; I triple checked to make sure everything was right and that there would be no way it would be postponed or cancelled.

Leading up to the surgery, there was one thing constantly on my mind: *What do I do afterward? What comes next?*

I asked my therapist this and her response was, "You enjoy it."

Those words helped me decide what I was going to do next. I knew this wasn't the end, that the surgery wasn't going to be a cure-all, but it was going to be an opportunity to go out and be the best possible version of myself.

My parents and I had to fly out of state for surgery. My mom came up with me for the first week I was in recovery and traded off with my dad during the second. When I went to the hospital in the early morning, it was hard to believe I was finally there. I went through some basic checkups before surgery and I kept worrying that something was going to go wrong and I would have to reschedule. The last thing I remember before going under was being wheeled into the surgery room and the next thing I knew, I was in a hospital room, loopy from the anesthesia. I spent the next few days just laying down, knowing I needed to rest but eager to see how everything was and to start walking.

I honestly didn't fully feel the difference emotionally until a week later, when I saw myself for the first time. At that moment, everything finally felt right. A huge wave of relief and happiness washed over me. For the first time in my life,

I felt like I was fully myself. I finally had the confidence in myself to do everything I had been afraid of doing because of my body, and I was going to take every opportunity to make sure I enjoyed it. After fighting to get to this point, I wanted to make the most of it.

HELPING OTHERS SHARE THEIR STORIES

Shortly after I had surgery, I graduated from college, and everything felt like it was at a standstill. After the activism I had done in college, I wanted to continue doing that meaningful work. I decided to move across the state to Orlando. I only knew a few people in the area, and it felt like I was starting over again. I tried to find work with a few different organizations, but unfortunately nothing panned out. I was left trying to decide where to go, what my plan was, and what I wanted to do.

Out of the blue, I got a text message from my cousin that he had met a trans woman at a bar, and he had mentioned me to her. He connected the two of us and that is how Ashley T Brundage (one of the contributors to this book) became a mentor to me and connected me with organizations in the area. That led me to a few networking events, and through a chance encounter at one such event, someone approached me as I was getting ready to leave and asked what I did. I told him I was newly graduated and a writer, and he introduced me to his friend, Dina. She introduced me electronically to Jenn T. Grace, the Founder and CEO of Publish Your Purpose Press.

When Jenn and I connected, she told me she was looking for some administrative help. I was excited to work for a business that shares my mission, to uplift diverse people's stories and raise their voices. In our initial conversation, I mentioned that I was a writer, and after working at Publish Your Purpose for some time, Jenn approached me about writing blog posts. I was ecstatic that I was able to write again, and shortly after that, she brought this book idea to me.

I was immediately onboard, more than happy to have the chance to help the contributors tell their stories and to share my story with you. It's been an incredible journey and, through this, things came full circle. Ashley reached out to ask for help creating and finishing her own book, *Empowering Differences*. I was excited to be asked and grateful to help her complete her book.

Through many conversations Ashley and I had, she empowered and encouraged me to start my own business, Best Laid Pens, whose mission is to help people share their stories and uplift the voices of people in my communities. That is what I plan to do through my writing and through my business.

Five years ago, I never would have imagined that this would be the path I'd carve for myself. Back in 2016, I didn't know where I was going or where I might end up but I'm happy with where I am now. I'm able to look at myself and think about all that I've overcome since I was young. I'm still enjoying every second of being my authentic self and sharing the stories of others as well as my own. No one can dictate the path I walk now.

My advice for any trans and nonbinary people reading this is that your story, your journey is your own. You have to make the decisions that work for you. The best time to be authentically you is now. Start being yourself, in whatever capacity you are able to. There are going to be hard choices that you'll need to make in your journey, and that's why you also need to find your community. Surround yourself with people who love you, care for you, and support you. Whether that is in person or online, a community will help uplift you. They will be the ones you lean on when you need it most and will support you when you make those decisions for yourself. It's never easy, but it's always worth it. Always remember that you were put on this earth because you are strong enough to make it.

Brandi Lai

INVISIBLE **STORIES**
WRITE TO BE SEEN

LISTEN TO THE *INVISIBLE STORIES* PODCAST

Have you always wanted to write a memoir or a book about your business but never started—or never finished that draft you set aside? If you're a business owner, speaker, or entrepreneur burning to tell your story, this podcast is for you. Writing a book can be a slow, painful process. It can even open old wounds and unearth memories that are difficult to share.

In this podcast, you'll hear inspiring interviews with published authors who are striving to make a difference in the world. You'll learn how they overcame self-doubt and past hurt to speak their truth...and how their book opened the doors to a wider audience, making a bigger impact than they ever thought was possible. The world deserves to hear your story—and you deserve the chance to tell it.

We urge you to share your story with us. Email us at
hello@publishyourpurpose.com and maybe
we'll include your story on our website. By sharing
your story with the world, you can feel a
sense of relief while helping others.

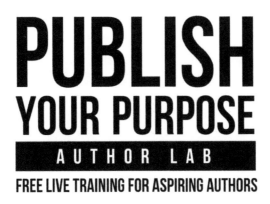

JOIN OUR FREE AUTHOR COMMUNITY

Hopeful. Energized. Inspired. These are just a few words used by our growing community of aspiring authors.

Are you ready to write and publish your book?

Are you overwhelmed about where to start? So much so that you are frozen in fear, prohibited from taking any action forward?

Have you been pushing this off for months, maybe even years?

If you want to do this, and are committed to doing this, then we are here to make it easier for you.

Take a moment and join our
free community on Facebook by either going to
www.meetthepublisher.com/authorlab or by typing
"Publish Your Purpose Author Lab" into Facebook.

GETTING STARTED
for AUTHORS

GET STARTED TELLING YOUR STORY

One of the hardest parts of writing a book is sitting down and getting started. That's why we've created the Getting Started for Authors program. This program focuses on four key areas of your writing process, including mindset, accountability, organization, and writing.

We will work hand in hand with you to get your manuscript written and ready for publishing. We meet weekly for book strategy sessions, writing sessions, and peer review and critique. The best part about having a community is knowing that you aren't on this journey alone.

To learn more about our next class, please visit
www.GettingStartedForAuthors.com.

If you have any questions, please reach out to us at
hello@publishyourpurpose.com.

ABOUT PUBLISH YOUR PURPOSE

Publish Your Purpose is a hybrid publisher of non-fiction books. Our mission is to elevate the voices often excluded from traditional publishing. We intentionally seek out authors and storytellers with diverse backgrounds, life experiences, and unique perspectives to publish books that will make an impact in the world. At PYP, we are fully invested in, and committed to, the success of our authors. We are focused on building long-term author relationships, not just business transactions.

We understand that publishing a book can be difficult. We go to great lengths to not only ensure your book is on track and meeting its deadline, but we also do our very best to manage your emotional overwhelm. Our work will enable you to maintain a clear focus on your vision. We act as your compass to ensure you get to your end goal.

Publish Your Purpose is a proud certified B Corporation, signifying that we meet rigorous standards of social and envi-ronmental performance, accountability, and transparency. PYP is also a certified woman-owned and LGBTQ-owned organization.

You can follow us on social media at—

www.YouTube.com/c/PublishYourPurpose
www.Twitter.com/PublishPurpose
www.Facebook.com/PublishYourPurpose
www.Instagram.com/PublishYourPurpose

To learn more about Publish Your Purpose,
visit **www.PublishYourPurpose.com**.

Printed in the USA
CPSIA information can be obtained
at www.ICGtesting.com
LVHW052052221223
766874LV00057B/280/J